About Demos

Who we are

Demos is the think tank for everyday democracy. We believe everyone should be able to make personal choices in their daily lives that contribute to the common good. Our aim is to put this democratic idea into practice by working with organisations in ways that make them more effective and legitimate.

What we work on

We focus on six areas: public services; science and technology; cities and public space; people and communities; arts and culture; and global security.

Who we work with

Our partners include policy-makers, companies, public service providers and social entrepreneurs. Demos is not linked to any party but we work with politicians across political divides. Our international network – which extends across Eastern Europe, Scandinavia, Australia, Brazil, India and China – provides a global perspective and enables us to work across borders.

How we work

Demos knows the importance of learning from experience. We test and improve our ideas in practice by working with people who can make change happen. Our collaborative approach means that our partners share in the creation and ownership of new ideas.

What we offer

We analyse social and political change, which we connect to innovation and learning in organisations. We help our partners show thought leadership and respond to emerging policy challenges.

How we communicate

As an independent voice, we can create debates that lead to real change. We use the media, public events, workshops and publications to communicate our ideas. All our books can be downloaded free from the Demos website.

www.demos.co.uk

First published in 2007
© Demos
Some rights reserved – see copyright licence for details

ISBN-10 1 84180 179 8
ISBN-13 978 1 84180 179 7

Copy edited by Julie Pickard, London
Typeset by utimestwo, Collingtree, Northants
Printed by IPrint, Leicester

For further information and
subscription details please contact:

Demos
Magdalen House
136 Tooley Street
London SE1 2TU

telephone: 0845 458 5949
email: hello@demos.co.uk
web: www.demos.co.uk

The Collaborative State

State

How working together can
transform public services

Edited by
Simon Parker
Niamh Gallagher

DEM⊙S

DEM©S

Contents

Contents

Collaboration in action

Redesigning the system

Acknowledgements

We are grateful to the National College for School Leadership and The Innovation Unit for supporting this work. In particular, we would like to thank David Jackson and Gene Payne – formerly of the college and now working with the IU – for their patience, support and encouragement throughout the project process.

Thanks are also due to the many talented and generous people who made the time to contribute essays, including those whose work has appeared on the project's website.

Many others have helped to produce and edit this collection. Tom Bentley put the project together, shepherded it through its early stages and provided thoughtful advice and support throughout. Molly Webb created the wiki pages that allowed us to publish and collaboratively edit much of the content. Peter Harrington and Julie Pickard managed the production process. Jamie Bartlett, Charlie Edwards and Guy Lodge kindly provided comments on early drafts.

Simon Parker
Niamh Gallagher
March 2007

Foreword

David Jackson and Gene Payne

It is now almost four years since Demos produced its highly influential and provocative publication *The Adaptive State*. It set out what proved to be an eloquent manifesto for public service reform. *The Adaptive State* was built not on the historical practice models and language of command, control, delivery and accountability but instead embraced new learning and adaptive models founded on principles of interdependence, collaborative practice, co-development, disciplined innovation, personalisation and shared narratives in the pursuit of public value.

If thought leadership from think tanks can help to shunt an entire system forward, then that publication did, and the extent to which this is the case is evident from the familiarity in 2007 not just of a new language of public service adaptation, but also of multiple operational images of practice across services, sectors and states.

In the intervening years, both The Innovation Unit and the National College for School Leadership have pioneered radical 'development and research' programmes in order to explore aspirational models of 'next practice' in networked learning and system leadership. Two of these are represented in this anthology among the many contributions from other sectors. That experience – one which inevitably takes education into change dialogues and partnerships laterally with other sectors and vertically with intermediate agencies and national policy processes – led to discussions with Demos about sponsoring a successor publication, *The Collaborative State*. Its suggested purpose was to map the evolution of thinking since its predecessor and to identify rich case studies from a range of public services in different jurisdictions which might offer examples and ideas for wider system learning.

We are delighted that we chose to support such a publication. It provides a stimulating, challenging and illuminating range of contributions, both accessible theory and models of replicable practice (if suitably adapted for purpose and context, of course). More importantly, it moves the debate forward in bringing to life new principles and emergent 'norms' for radical public service reform. If *Adaptive State* offered the confidence to utilise new principles and a new language, *Collaborative State* is more challenging. In offering compelling arguments and examples of success built on trust relationships, shared accountabilities, social justice imperatives and co-design practices that empower the users that public services serve, it is an exhortation to action.

Put like that, we are proud to support it!

David Jackson and Gene Payne are consultants on The Innovation Unit's next practice programmes. They were previously directors at the National College for School Leadership.

Introduction

Simon Parker and Niamh Gallagher

In Knowsley, nearly two-thirds of 14–16-years-olds spend some of their time learning outside their school,[1] while their teachers carry out secondments and peer reviews aimed at sharing ideas and creating higher expectations. In Kent, the county council's chief executive regularly sits down with 12 other key players to try and coordinate public spending across the whole area.[2] At a seminar in London, the Audit Commission's Mark Wardman produces mind-bendingly complicated maps of all the organisations involved in reducing obesity. Some public sector partnerships, he points out, can contain as many as 50 different players.[3]

Seen in isolation, these are just one-off examples of useful joint working – the kind of thing good public servants have always done. Taken together, they are part of a major trend that is challenging the way governments traditionally do business. A wave of experimentation with collaborative government has been unleashed since the late 1990s which has seen administrations from Finland to New Zealand launching new initiatives for joined-up government, local partnerships, place-based policy-making and the co-production and design of services with the public. These innovations could be the key to a new wave of public service reform.

Common sense, the evidence base, perhaps even our genetic code tells us that collaboration makes sense. The big, complex social problems that governments want to address – from crime and security to poverty and health – simply cannot be tackled within the fragmented public sector delivery systems that have resulted from over a century of bureaucracy and decades of competitive reform.

These problems have multiple causes, and those causes often interact in unpredictable ways. Attack just one and you are liable to be thwarted by the others. So governments need to be able to act on many fronts at once if they want to attempt a solution. And that in turn means increasingly that an active social policy can come only from multiple organisations working together with the people they serve, achieving things that no organisation or individual could alone.

At the very least, this kind of collaboration offers governments a way to expand their social ambitions in a consensual way. Collaboration between organisations offers a way to weld different services and agencies into a more coherent problem-solving whole without tying them into rigid new structures. Collaboration between citizens and public institutions offers new ways to engage the public in keeping themselves healthy, or tackle anti-social behaviour, but it also allows people to opt out of the process if they so wish. Sir Michael Lyons hints at this approach in his call for councils to become strategic 'place shapers' – convening and shaping collaborations across whole local areas.

But at best, collaboration holds out the tantalising prospect of a new approach to running local public services. It presents the possibility of replacing the old rigidities with flexible federations of public bodies that can quickly sense and adapt to changing need, at the same time creating new forums that bring people and institutions together to identify shared problems and work collaboratively on solutions.

Despite some brave innovations, we have barely begun to test the potential of collaboration as a design principle for public service reform. This collection mixes leading-edge case studies with more scholarly essays in an attempt to understand how far we have come and where we might go next. Its three sections ask the questions: Why work together? Where can the beginnings of new approaches be found? And what would government look like if we redesigned it for collaboration?

These are pressing issues for the UK's public services. Over the past 20 years, successive governments have driven through reforms based on inspection, markets and contractualism. These have driven swift and predictable improvements, but increasingly they seem to be delivering diminishing returns. Evidence is beginning to suggest that the current reform programme is improving services while simultaneously reducing public trust.[4] And you need only look at the bewildering range of agencies working in any given locality to see that tight contractual control has come at the expense of fragmentation.

Competition and choice are vital tools, but they are not enough. If we want to engage the public in solving social problems, if we want public services that add up to more than the sum of their parts, and if we want a more open and democratic set of institutions, then we need a new wave of change that starts with collaboration.

Why collaborate?

A cynic once described the rise of public sector partnerships as 'the suppression of mutual loathing in pursuit of government money'. The reality is that collaborative working offers more than Whitehall grants. Many of the contributors to this collection point to a powerful moral imperative among public servants for collaboration, but there are tangible benefits, too.

Creating new ways to solve complex social problems is, of course, the key driver. At its most simple, collaboration happens when groups of local healthcare professionals work with their patients to redesign a cancer service in Luton – a project described by Lynne Maher in chapter 8. On a grander scale, it might be about experiments such as the creation of the networked learning communities David Jackson describes in chapter 6 – collaborative groups of schools that have allowed areas like Knowsley to develop radically new service offerings since the early 2000s. Strategically, it is about generating collaborative systems that allow governments, citizens and civil society to shape whole economies and societies – something that governments in Wales and Australia are both attempting (chapters 4 and 5).

From local strategic partnerships to crime and disorder reduction schemes, collaboration has also created new spaces that encourage democratic engagement with the public. Citizens seldom understand their problems in terms that fit easily into state structures, and they seldom express their concerns in the antiseptic language of budgets and structures. They can engage in a far more meaningful and powerful way with the question of how services work together to create safer neighbourhoods than they can with individual consultations about the police, street cleansing and housing.

Moreover, local collaborations invariably involve a degree of bespoke decision-making about community needs, making partnerships places where policy is tailored and shaped, and creating more points of autonomy and negotiation.

Just as importantly, collaboration offers a new frontier in the government's search for greater efficiency within the public sector. By taking a whole system view of their interventions in local people's lives, bodies like local strategic partnerships can redesign local services around outcomes for the citizen, removing processes that don't contribute to solving problems, identifying duplication of effort and focusing resources on the people they serve.

Beyond the theory

So how far have we come towards a more collaborative kind of government? Experience varies according to country and sector – a fact reflected by the diversity of views included in this collection. But the resounding message is that while progress has been made, there is still a long way to go. As Sue Goss argues in chapter 2: 'While we don't yet in the UK have what we could describe as a "collaborative state", we have moved a long way from the single-agency delivery systems that existed only a decade ago.'

Collaboration has been slow to take hold in large part because it is easy in theory, but fiendishly difficult in practice. One recent study neatly sums up the literature with its argument that successful collaborative working needs to be based on a sense of shared purpose, high-level commitment from the organisations involved, trust and clarity of objectives.

And yet a third of interviewees for the same study also reported that the costs of working with others had outweighed the benefits.[5] The moral and practical goals of collaboration are too often undermined by failings that range from over-ambition and a weak sense of purpose to the difficulty of integrating the legacy of old functional and professional structures that remain within the public sector.

In a world focused on action and achievement, collaboration often seems like a distraction from completing tasks and meeting output targets. Worse, for professional groups collaboration can sometimes suggest a betrayal of their training, values and identities as they take on responsibilities traditionally associated with others. There are also a number of 'hidden' attitudinal barriers to collaboration that Henry Tam argues need to be addressed – from the tendency of some public servants to put innovation before people to the 'postmodern feudal barons' who are interested in new initiatives only if they can take the credit.

But not all the barriers lie in the locality – effective collaboration is also frustrated by rigid, confused and contradictory policy from the centre. Seen from the town hall, government departments can often appear to be lumbering beasts more interested in meeting political targets than really solving local problems. Frontline collaboration easily becomes stifled by fragmented budgets, narrowly focused inspections and targets that somehow don't add up on the ground. Joining up services around local needs is very difficult when the providers of those services are busy trying to meet targets often unilaterally designed by the centre. As Geoff Mulgan, former head of the prime minister's strategy unit, has pointed out:

> The old departmental traditions remain very strong. The great majority of budgets and policy processes [are] still organised within old structures. Most ministers still primarily interpret

their roles in vertical ways. . . . Some of the work of coordination remains excessively time-consuming because structures have not been reformed.[6]

Of course, these problems often look very different from Whitehall. Collaborative approaches by their nature involve local public servants tailoring their services to local needs, raising the danger of postcode lotteries and creating a lack of information about what's really happening on the ground. Collaboration also creates murky accountabilities – is a fall in crime due to the local authority's neighbourhood wardens, a new policy from a local housing association or more effective police action, or a combination of all three of these? And who gets the blame when something goes wrong? All of which raises a deeper set of questions of not just how, but by whom the public sector is held accountable.

Why cause and effect matters

The Harvard Business School academics Clayton Christensen, Matthew Marx and Howard Stevenson make the simple but persuasive argument that effective collaboration hinges on two key factors: a shared sense of what people want to achieve and some degree of consensus on cause and effect – the things that will allow them to achieve it.[7] Where there are high levels of agreement on both, then the establishment of traditions, rituals and democratic processes becomes the best way to link people who fundamentally share the same aims – both within organisations and between them and the people they serve. Management becomes easier, more collaborative and more consensual.

Seen from this perspective, the real failure of Labour's approach over the past decade has been in establishing a shared sense of cause and effect. Febrile reform of institutions like the NHS has often bred confusion and resentment about the best means to the end of a healthier population, particularly as the government's preferred means – markets and performance indicators – often seem to threaten cherished professional values and autonomy.

The approach that the National College for School Leadership took to implementing networked learning communities (NLCs) might provide important lessons for a more effective model of change than the constant upheaval of the past decade. The NLC programme was built on a set of values that were widely shared across the teaching profession – all children had potential if they could be taught well, and the key to doing that was to work across organisational boundaries to provide a richer education experience. In the process, they could share practice, find economies of scale and innovate together.

Interestingly, the collaborative work took place in a context of choice for parents and competition between schools for resources. The important thing as we enter an era of trust schools will be to find the optimum combination of these two principles, rather than being forced to make a false choice between them.

In chapter 6 David Jackson describes the NLCs as a 'design intervention' – there was basic documentation and plenty of support for school leaders, but little prescription from the centre. The point was to help people develop their own arrangements and relationships. The programme did provide some money, but this had to be matched by the schools themselves as a sign of commitment. There were no onerous audits, but external evaluations were carried out after two years and the learning communities were encouraged to practise self- and peer-review. The key thing was to encourage learning and development.

As that suggests, the moral imperative to collaborate can be a powerful driver of change, but only when it is nurtured, supported and incentivised in ways that resonate with public servants themselves. The benefit of NLCs was that they tapped into a shared sense of vision, but allowed maximum space for local groups to develop their own sense of cause and effect. Public policy cannot always be this consensual, but if it harnessed professional knowledge, values and expertise we would take a big step towards a more collaborative state.

The next stage: system redesign

The great contest in the public sector between competitive market, collaborative network and bureaucratic hierarchy probably does not end with a victory for any one kind of organisation. That would simply replace one form of structural headache with another. The more desirable outcome is a truce, in which government looks like a matrix of relatively independent service deliverers glued together by collaboratively developed central government policies and stronger kinds of horizontal coordination on the ground. Problem-solving networks will not become new permanent organisations, but shifting sets of projects that are able to reconfigure themselves rapidly to meet changing local and national needs.

That kind of world will not emerge solely through more structural change and legislation – central policy-making might be able to force the appearance of collaboration, but it can only try to catalyse the emergent and messy reality. Genuine collaboration will have to evolve through a journey of evolution and learning, supported by real commitment from local services and central government. That process could be sped up considerably if our public service systems were redesigned to encourage collaboration. On the evidence of this collection, four kinds of change are necessary:

O   Central government needs to become more collaborative
    in the way it makes and implements policy, working with
    frontline staff to develop shared visions and allowing
    more space for experimentation with cause and effect.
O   Policy-makers need to create targets, accountabilities and
    assessment systems based around broad outcome goals.
O   Local service providers need to develop a new generation
    of collaborative 'system leaders' who can broker and
    manage joint working across local areas.
O   Citizens and frontline public servants need to develop
    more opportunities and greater capacity for collaboration,
    driving co-production and co-design.

Central government can start by honestly appraising its own approach to collaboration – chapter 13 argues that Whitehall should experiment with its own cross-departmental policy networks, involving wide networks of key practitioners in forming and implementing strategy. Ministers and civil servants need to become less reliant on trying to force change through legislation and new duties. Instead, it should find new ways to set the agenda by focusing the effort of public service systems on particular problems and cooperate with delivery systems to guide and augment their existing work.

The moral imperative to collaborate is a powerful motivation, but it needs support and incentivisation. Central targets need to be set in ways that encourage local agencies to work together, with national goals becoming ever fewer, broader and more strategic. Judgements of an area's success need to be based on whether or not the whole system of local service provision is meeting long-term outcome goals – a healthier population, safer streets or a more successful economy. If success was increasingly judged by local people, that would also provide a powerful driver for local services to join up around citizens rather than national goals.

At the local level, current efforts at collaboration need to become deeper and more serious attempts at joint strategy-making and problem-solving, increasingly involving the public and other sectors as empowered partners. Leadership matters immensely in this process. As Valerie Hannon points out in chapter 11, local organisations need to encourage, develop and reward their 'system leaders' – those rare individuals who are expert at delivering their own excellent services, but can also lead groups of organisations towards shared goals.

These managers need to be capable of seeing the whole system of provision, and of generating the legitimacy to make trade-offs between different organisations and goals. We need to develop professional training and development offerings that create more of them and that instil a shared sense of ethos and purpose across the public service workforce.

But collaboration is not just a matter for leaders. We also need to develop greater capacity for frontline public servants to work with the people they serve to co-design and co-produce services. As Sophia Parker argues in chapter 15, creating more opportunities for direct participation is important – neighbourhood committees and foundation trusts are useful developments – but we cannot rely on this as a sole strategy. We also need to enlist the voluntary sector as a partner in building the capability and willingness of the public to collaborate. Finally, we can use indirect ways of engaging people, using service design techniques to see services as citizens do and driving innovation in the process.

If governments cannot manage more innovative and collaborative approaches to social problems, there is growing evidence that their citizens can. As Paul Miller and Niamh Gallagher show in their study of katrinalist.net in chapter 9, the internet is increasingly enabling people to respond to their own problems far more quickly than the state can. This is perhaps the most disruptive development that we cover in this book. Yale University's Yochai Benkler argues that networked collaboration between members of the public might ultimately mean that 'there is more freedom to be found through opening up institutional spaces for voluntary individual and cooperative action than there is in intentional public action through the state'.[8]

If he is right, then collaboration between individuals themselves could make both the state and the market look very different over the coming years.

Simon Parker is head of public services research at Demos. Niamh Gallagher is a researcher at Demos.

Notes

1   More details on Knowsley can be found at www.ncsl.org.uk/media/C55/2E/lea-project-case-study-knowsley.pdf (accessed 19 Feb 2007).
2   More details can be found at www.kentpartnership.org.uk/public-service-board.asp (accessed 19 Feb 2007).
3   See, for instance, Audit Commission, *Governing Partnerships: Bridging the*

accountability gap (London: Audit Commission, 2005) available at
http://icn.csip.org.uk/_library%2FResources%2FSupport_materials%2FGover
ning%20Partnerships%20-%20Bridging%20the%20accountability%20Gap.pdf
(accessed 9 Mar 2007).

4   P Taylor-Gooby, 'The efficiency/trust dilemma', *Health, Risk and Society* 8, no 2
     (2006).

5   Hay Group, *Decisive Collaboration and the Rise of Networked Professionalism*
     (London: Hay Group, July 2006) available from
     www.haygroup.com/uk/Research/Detail.asp?PageID=2922 (accessed 9 Mar
     2007).

6   G Mulgan, *Joined up Government: Past, present and future* (London: Young
     Foundation, 2005), available at www.youngfoundation.org.uk/node/223
     (accessed 19 Feb 2007).

7   CM Christensen, M Marx and HH Stevenson, 'The tools of cooperation and
     change', *Harvard Business Review*, Oct 2006.

8   Y Benkler, *The Wealth of Networks* (London: Yale University Press, 2006).

Essay summaries

Collaboration as design principle
Beyond state and market: social cooperation as a new domain of policy
Yochai Benkler

The rise of social production in the networked information economy has shown that the binary state–market conception that typified twentieth-century economic and policy thought is at best a partial understanding of the range of options for effective social action. We are seeing individuals and groups of all shapes and forms beginning to take advantage of networked communications to form collaborative networks, sharing effort and material resources in decentralised networks to solve problems once thought amenable only to centralised control. These approaches are not an aberration, but are at the core of what happens when human beings are entrusted with the capacity and authority to act together to improve their lot.

How far have we travelled towards a collaborative state?
Sue Goss

We have moved a long way from the single-agency delivery systems that existed only a decade ago, but there is still scope to take collaborative working further – reconfiguring services radically across boundaries to generate new sorts of provision. In the private sector, there is now talk of 'chaordic' organisations, which are primarily networks operating with fluid delivery but strong governance. These sorts of models are even more likely to be needed in the public sector. The next challenge is to design approaches to governance that can secure strong legitimacy and accountability in modern, transparent interactive terms for networks of organisations that are fluid and creative.

Roots of cooperation and routes to collaboration
Barry Quirk

There are substantial benefits to be gained in collaboration across public organisations – to build public value as well as to reduce costs. But the management agenda of sharing service costs, aggregating demand and supply and reducing overheads does not describe the totality of the possible. A wider civic purpose pervades democratic local government. Councils will attain the position marked out for them in the Lyons report only if they collaborate in 360 degrees – with their citizens, with local businesses, with suppliers and service partners, and with their own staff.

The conditions for collaboration: early learning from Wales
Steve Martin and Adrian Webb

Wales wants to use collaboration as a principle for reshaping its public services. Making a reality of that aspiration requires a fundamental change in central government's role – away from a preoccupation with policy formulation and reliance on arm's length command and control towards a much greater focus on delivery and 'engaged leadership' of managed networks of service providers. Local agencies will need to be much more willing to work together. Central and local government will have to develop mechanisms for pooling resources and accountability in respect of key outcomes.

Working together for stronger Victorian communities
Yehudi Blacher and David Adams

The idea of collaboration is now well entrenched in public policy, yet the actual administrative arrangements necessary to give effect to the idea are still emerging. In this case study we canvass the 'organising' aspects that give administrative form to collaboration. We do this through the lens of the Victorian government's community-strengthening strategy – since to be effective, community strengthening requires substantial collaboration with communities, with other departments and with other sectors.

Collaboration in action
Networked learning communities: collaboration by design
David Jackson

In education, there is an increasingly widespread view that a more collaborative, adaptive and long-term problem-solving approach is the way to go. Getting there requires a different model of change: one which emphasises capacity-building, which spreads and uses leadership widely, which enables and encourages rapid knowledge transfer, which fosters and utilises practitioner innovation and creativity, which values system learning and builds for sustainability. The problem is we just don't yet know how to orchestrate such a pervasive change.

Learning together: the collaborative college
Sarah Gillinson, Celia Hannon and Niamh Gallagher

Without collaboration, Lewisham College would never be able to reach young people in the local community, including the large numbers who were either excluded from school, or who stayed but were seriously demotivated by the experience. And without strong links to the 'real world' of business, the college would find it much harder to help those young people into good jobs.

Your experience matters: designing healthcare with citizens
Lynne Maher

Luton and Dunstable Hospital has taken a collaborative approach to the ongoing redesign of its head and neck cancer service by putting patients and staff right at the centre of the process. Using the concept of 'experience-based design', patients and carers are invited to tell stories about their experience of the service. These stories provide insights that enable the designers to think about designing better experiences, rather than just designing services.

Katrina's code: how online collaboration came to the rescue in New Orleans
Paul Miller and Niamh Gallagher

On 29 August 2005, Hurricane Katrina decimated the American city of New Orleans. The storm ripped through the region, causing the worst natural disaster in living memory. Outside the structures and agencies of government, the lack of reliable information led to the creation of some unusual solutions that might point to new forms of collaboration for the future. For the first time, online tools were used in a concerted way by concerned citizens to help the victims of a major disaster.

Policing the front line
Charlie Edwards

A new approach to policing is taking hold in Oxford. It relies heavily on partnerships between the police, communities, local businesses and other public services. The logic is simple – the police recognise that they can create safe communities only if they work with a wide variety of other public services. The approach is promising, but it will work only if the government recognises the importance of local priority setting, and if local public services are themselves bold enough to shift responsibility away from managers in the town hall to frontline staff.

New leadership for the collaborative state
Valerie Hannon

The commonly held, professionally respectable approach of most teachers in the new century is to acknowledge the interconnectedness of their actions. To a greater or lesser extent, they accept the implications of what they do for other schools. School leaders increasingly aspire to take on the responsibility for all the learners in their local area, but while considerable strides have been made in that direction, there are still a lot of road blocks. This essay describes some of those road blocks and sets out why innovative approaches to leadership are needed in such a context.

Overcoming the hidden barriers
Henry Tam

For every success story of collaboration, there are joint enterprises that came to a halt because one or more hidden barriers to collaboration had made progress impossible. Without going directly into the sensitive territories of reviewing these cases, we can consider the lessons from them by examining the generic features of these barriers. There are four key issues: the imperial court syndrome; the pseudo-diversity trap; the innovations-first/citizens-last complex; and the postmodern feudal barons.

Redesigning the system
Beyond delivery: a collaborative Whitehall
Simon Parker

The traditional models of governing are becoming less powerful, so governments need to explore new methods that do not so much seek to deliver things, as to determine goals and direction, provide resources and broker relationships that allow others to do their jobs. To lead whole systems of public service provision, central government departments themselves need to become more collaborative, encouraging department to work with department, but also connecting civil servants more effectively to the outside world of delivery.

Flesh, steel and Wikipedia: how government can make the most of online collaborative tools
Paul Miller and Molly Webb

At the moment the idea of millions of people collaborating for the public good using technology seems mind-boggling. But in the future it will be much less so, as we begin to understand the patterns and motivations of activity that are taking place in projects such as Wikipedia or the open source operating system Linux. The old 'cyberspace versus government' framing of the situation now needs to be replaced by a new understanding of the way that online tools could help government, and in helping government help the rest of us to live the lives we want to lead.

The co-production paradox
Sophia Parker

Co-production – the jargon for greater collaboration between the state and its citizens – is a vision for transformation, a recasting of the relationship between individuals and the world in which they live. At its best, deep collaboration between citizens and the state is about giving people a chance to play an active role in shaping their own lives. It is about enhancing what Robert Sampson has called collective efficacy – in other words, helping people to make connections between the decisions they make and the quality of the public realm.

Evolving the future
Tom Bentley

The collaborative state challenges many roles, powers and assumptions that have held for more than a century of modern government. Reformers are already seeking new routes through which to achieve large-scale change, and new models for collective provision in diverse societies. Collaboration, pursued with discipline, is the route to the redesign of our large-scale services and governance structures. The challenge of leadership is to focus on the problems that government exists to solve.

Collaboration as design principle

1. Beyond state and market

Social cooperation as a new domain of policy
Yochai Benkler

The past decade has seen a transformation in the organisation of production in the core sectors of the most advanced economies in the world. The adoption of networked personal computers and communications devices enabled radical decentralisation of the physical capital necessary to produce information, knowledge and culture. This decentralisation of capital allowed people to act in the economic domain by using practices previously reserved for the social domain.

In the days when what was good for GM was good for the United States, no matter how avid an automobile fanatic one may have been, one could not get together with friends on the weekend and produce cars in competition with General Motors. Now, as Microsoft has taken the place of GM, we do see increasing use of free and open source software, like the GNU/Linux operating system, which powers the servers of Google or Amazon, or the Apache Web Server software that handles the secure transactions of Deutschebank.

In the cultural domain, Wikipedia and the rise of citizen journalism have been the most visible examples of the rise of commons-based peer production: large-scale collaboration of individuals on information, knowledge and cultural production, without price signals, outside of the traditional managerial systems of the state and large organisations, and without resort to proprietary exclusion as the organising principle of production.

The rise of the networked information economy challenges our basic approach to policy. Responding to the demise of state socialism and rising anxieties over eurosclerosis in the 1980s, the last decade of the twentieth century saw a dramatic reconstruction of the centre-left political agenda.

Personified by the charisma of Tony Blair and Bill Clinton, New Labour and the New Democrats embraced market-based institutional innovation. From tradeable emissions for pollutants, through spectrum auctions in wireless communications, to managed competition as the solution to health coverage, the new centre-left embraced and adopted market-based mechanisms as the *primary* solution space for institutional innovation in contemporary societies.

The rise of social production in the networked information economy has shown that the binary state–market conception that typified twentieth-century economic and policy thought is at best a partial understanding of the range of options for effective social action. This is not to say that markets will suddenly be swept away. That would be silly to say and disastrous to live through.

Nor is it to say that the state has lost any role. That would be equally silly and disruptive. But these two do not exhaust the range of options for effective social practice. Instead, we are seeing individuals and groups of all shapes and forms beginning to take advantage of networked communications to form collaborative networks, sharing effort and material resources in decentralised networks to solve problems once thought amenable only to centralised control – by either regulators or property owners. Take an example from wireless policy.

For over half a century, economists have criticised the prevailing approach to wireless systems regulation. They argued instead for a market in spectrum allocations. In the past decade regulators the world over have taken heed, adopting spectrum auctions with a vengeance. Yet, just as this widespread embrace of a market mechanism for spectrum allocation was adopted, it became technologically obsolete.

Low computation costs and innovation in information theory and in network and antenna technology made reliance on distributed approaches, based on a commons-like treatment of 'the spectrum', both theoretically desirable and technically feasible. The most visible primitive instance are the WiFi networks becoming ubiquitous around the world. We are beginning to see local communities, sometimes through local government, often through volunteer efforts, provide an alternative local broadband network using this open spectrum.

Deregulation of spectrum can now take the form of permitting people to deploy cooperative wireless devices that comply with minimal safety rules – rather like automobiles – rather than forcing the creation of a market by prohibiting wireless emissions except with a licence purchased at auction. The result has been dramatic improvement in wireless internet access and the emergence of both market-based and non-market networks, all based on using the spectrum commons.

Wireless policy is an example, not a unique case. It represents the possibilities that open up when we abandon the simplistic state–market binary of policy solutions.

This binary view of policy has its roots in the view that human beings, left with the freedom to act alone or together, are selfish, calculating nasties. They must, so the thought goes, be ruled by government or provided with extrinsic 'incentives' through as near as perfect a market as feasible to get them to act in their own common good.

This is a profoundly distressing and demeaning view of humanity. And it is empirically unwarranted. Over a decade of research in experimental economics and game theory, anthropology and social psychology, neuroscience and human evolutionary biology all persistently point in the same direction.

No, we are not the self-sacrificing angels that utopian anarchists might once have imagined. But neither are we the nasty brutes of rational choice theory, Hobbesian political theory and market-based-everything advocates. Some of us are selfish, yes. Others, true altruists. Many of us are reciprocators. We meet kindness with kindness, and meanness with meanness. We cooperate with those who cooperate with us, and seek to punish those who abuse us. Given the opportunity, we can police ourselves and our social relations by finding trustworthy friends and cooperators, and keep wayward members more or less in line.

There is nothing earth shattering about this to anyone who has lived some portion of their lives with eyes open. It should not have taken hundreds of experiments, several competing theoretical frameworks, and thousands of academic papers to make the basic diversity of human motivation and proclivity to cooperate clear. We have too long laboured under a powerful and negative view of humanity as requiring either control or crass incentives in the form of extrinsic rewards and punishments for closely monitored behaviour. We can do better.

Social cooperation is not a magic wand to be waved at all problems. But one critical difference between left and right is the ability to see that markets, like states, are no panacea. Like the state, markets are made of fallible people and imperfect institutions. Like the state, with its corruptibility and periodic bouts of arrogance, markets and market actors too have their imperfections: their power, their blindness and their abuses.

No single system alone can optimise life, freedom and basic human wellbeing in complex contemporary human societies. Our experience with social cooperation on the network is too young to offer us any confidence that this new approach is, at long last, *the* one right solution. But social cooperation is offering us another degree of freedom in the design of human societies, another solution space to the problem of how to live together well.

This new cooperative approach need not be coded 'left' in the twentieth century sense. It is, largely, 'deregulatory' in its institutional forms. It depends on freely given cooperation among individuals. It should not, in principle, be unattractive to libertarians – and many libertarians indeed do embrace various regulatory positions – like open wireless spectrum, or a sceptical view of software patents – aimed at giving free reign to cooperation.

But there are many libertarians who are suspicious of the idea that people will simply volunteer to do things because they are the right thing to do, because they are socially fulfilling, and in any event not through a market transaction. The left and centre-left should have no such compunctions. We should approach any problem posed in terms of the market–state dichotomy with scepticism. We should look for, and be open to, designing systems that harness human cooperation where possible. In the networked information economy we see the power of social production everywhere.

Elsewhere, we are only beginning to learn that these approaches are not an aberration, but are rather at the core of what happens when human beings are entrusted with the capacity and authority to act together to improve their lot.

We need to insist on humanity and on our basic capacity to cooperate with each other freely. And we need to insist on it not merely as an ideal, but as a basic design element of human systems.

Yochai Benkler is professor of law at Yale Law School.

2. How far have we travelled towards a collaborative state?

Sue Goss

While we don't yet in the UK have what we could describe as a 'collaborative state', we have moved a long way from the single-agency delivery systems that existed only a decade ago. In this essay I want to look at the distance that has been travelled, the obstacles that remain, and the path the journey might yet take.

Ironically, it was the fragmentation of public services during the 1980s and 1990s that meant collaboration became essential if anything was to get done. Many services that were previously run by local or central government were handed over to next steps agencies, quangos or private and voluntary sector providers; the funding of further education was transferred to the learning and skills councils; economic development and business support became the job of regional development agencies; central government services were managed through next steps agencies; 80 per cent of social care was expected to come from the private and voluntary sector; and housing was transferred to housing associations and ALMOs (arm's length management organisations). Government provision was 'hollowed out' and delivery systems multiplied. At the same time globalisation meant that geographical areas were becoming far more interdependent. The emergence of single job markets within city regions like London or greater Manchester, for instance, means that local authorities, or even health authorities, can't work alone. And as the role of local government begins to be seen not simply as the provision of a bundle of services – but about 'place shaping' and the delivery of outcomes rather than outputs – single service or organisational silos won't do.

Collaborative working is not without cost, however. It is far, far harder to deliver through collaborative action than through a single agency. It takes far longer to achieve things through agreement – partnerships have weaker power of 'agency' than single agencies. A partnership remains 'inert', unable to command or deploy resources, unless decisions are linked directly into the delivery systems of participating organisations. At the same time, partnerships offer the possibilities of breaking out of the assumptions and constraints that 'lock' member agencies into traditional solutions – they offer the potential of 'unoccupied' or 'experimental' space where organisational obstacles and 'group think' are less strong. Those involved in partnerships see the potential and experience the frustration. Often people involved in, or observing, collaborative working feel that the enormous amount of effort involved, with relatively little to show for it, makes partnerships net consumers of value rather than value creators. In one county council partnership conference we covered a wall with the names of the different partnerships across the county – all of them together involving hundreds of organisations. All this consumes considerable resource.

Yet few people disputed the need for them. The alternatives are worse. While it would, in theory, be possible to try and redraw organisational boundaries instead, this simply creates as many problems as it solves. Endless reorganisation through the cycle of centralisation and decentralisation – trying to get the delivery architecture 'right' – leads to the discovery that there is no 'right' structure. Organisations that are large enough to be strategic are always too large to be intimately connected to consumers; or they are small enough to be engaged closely with communities but too small to carry the power and leverage to make change happen. Bringing children's services together integrates in one way, but creates new separations between adult and children's social services. Most practitioners can see that partnerships are the only realistic game in town.

Indeed, what is surprising is the practical success that is being achieved in partnership working. On the ground, functioning partnerships between health and social care deliver more or less integrated services – partnerships design and develop children's services; youth offending teams involve police, social services and the criminal justice professionals; and community safety partnerships plan interventions to reduce crime. In virtually every area of the country we can find successful examples of collaboration – consortia of public agencies providing shared services, neighbouring local authorities using each other's legal or public relations departments, large-scale partnerships between local authorities and private sector companies to provide the 'front end' of service delivery, shared offices between health and social services departments, collaborative multi-disciplinary teams, police officers based in schools and local authority staff based in hospitals.

At the very local level, practical initiatives such as Sure Start, anti-obesity initiatives and economic development projects are all organised on a collaborative basis. In one area, for example, the chief executive of the primary care trust is also the director of social services for the local authority; in another area the borough commander has joined the top management team of the local authority. Where boundaries are shared, partnerships have been able to align resources and spending plans; even when boundaries are different, creative agencies have been able to create new teams coterminous with local authorities so that teams of staff can work alongside each other. In some areas we are moving towards the creation of a management team for the whole locality capable of looking at all the problems together.

So far, so good. But because public services are based on collective decision-making and democratic accountability, the integration of delivery systems inevitably means rethinking governance. Since 1997, this has been explicitly part of the government's partnership agenda, through the development of Local Strategic Partnerships (LSPs) responsible in each area for the development of a community strategy – later called a Sustainable Community Strategy – which spells out the needs of each locality, and the action that will be taken to meet them. Through Local Public Service Agreements, which begin a contractual negotiation between localities and the centre around stretch targets, other public agencies began to be linked into plans which were geographically, rather than nationally, focused. Local Area Agreements carry this forward – now in each locality key public sector agencies come together under the umbrella of the LSP to develop shared outcomes and shared targets, and to align their plans and resources to meet them.

The local government white paper[1] and the report of the Lyons Inquiry[2] are expected to reinforce this approach.

We need to step back a moment, and remember what a radical change of understanding this is about how government works and how decisions are taken. Instead of each local agency being expected to provide a range of local services, the local authority is asked to lead a partnership of agencies – working closely with the wider community – to understand and meet the needs of a place. Making this change has been slower and more painful than some in both national and local government envisaged – but why anyone would have expected such an entirely new approach to government, service delivery and decision-making to work simply and easily is a mystery!

In the first place, the expectation is that different sorts of legitimacy and accountability can be 'pooled' effectively. In reality this has proved terribly hard. The local authority, for example, carries legitimacy derived from local democratic elections, and is therefore primarily responsible outwards to the local electorate. Nevertheless, they are also funded by central government to provide a range of services to standards that are often centrally set and independently monitored. Other public sector agencies gain their legitimacy from their accountability upwards – to ministers – and therefore feel constrained by targets and goals set by the centre. While these individual lines of accountability are often strong, collective accountability in partnerships is relatively weak.

For the voluntary sector, community sector, faith groups and business – the issue of their role in community decision-making is even more complex – since while they have been chosen for their different perspectives, they can't be said to authoritatively 'speak for' all the sections of the wider community, and can't be held to account for their decisions. Community representatives need to negotiate their own legitimacy and come to terms with the role they play and the extent to which they are 'authorised' to act for others. Business representatives can begin to feel very uncomfortable about the idea of being 'held to account' for the actions of the partnership.

Meanwhile, local politicians respond in a number of different ways – some see the huge potential of effective partnerships and see their role as leading through effective partnerships; directly elected mayors and council leaders can see their role transformed from 'leading the council' to 'leading the city'. For others, however, and often for backbenchers, there is a worry that power is leaching away from democratically elected structures into more shadowy and less accountable partnerships.

Partnership working, therefore, tends to be based on the assumption that a consensus can be found, and that with enough hard work, all the interests in a locality will be discovered to be congruent. In reality, however, there may be conflicting interests and conflicting priorities – even between agencies scarce resources may mean a fight as to which projects are funded – and resource decisions have to be taken between different parts of a city or county, between urban and rural areas, between the most deprived and the areas most capable of renewal, between the young and the old, between the poor and the middle classes. The temptation, then, is for community strategies and partnership plans to remain relatively general and bland, to sustain a loose consensus. When hard choices need to be faced, partnerships either 'borrow' the democratic legitimacy of the local authority, or accept the imposed priorities of central government. For partnerships in two-tier areas, however, this often proves very difficult.

Partnership working can also challenge the sense of purpose carried by each agency, and the identity of the professionals within each service is often closely bound up with their particular perspective on client groups and how their problems and issues are understood and addressed. Collaborative work requires professionals to acknowledge the perspective of others as equally valid, and in some cases this can be experienced as a threat to identity and expertise.

Often there is a clash between the evidence base of public agencies, and the views and perceptions of local people. The strong evidence base which drives partnerships can be a powerful antidote to myth and prejudice – but at the same time, agencies need to learn to listen to the experiences of local people. A plurality of views and representatives can become an active strength, using the creative tension between the different styles and viewpoints of the different constituent parts – different 'ways of seeing' – as a way to make breakthroughs and find new solutions. Rather than see this as a problem, an LSP can operate as a place where two important sources of ideas come together – the evidence and data of the public sector organisations, and the views, preferences and experiences of the community, voluntary and business sectors.

This would mean organising partnership working to maximise that 'collision of ideas' but to do so within relationships and ways of working that are able to find serious debate energising and resolve conflict. Instead of elected representatives or nationally driven agencies simply imposing solutions, this creates the possibility of solutions negotiated with different communities and interest groups. Instead of conflict between different professional perspectives it offers the possibility that the debate between them could generate more creative approaches. All this, however, requires that the partnership is set up in ways that enable this creative process to take place. And none of this can be taken to mean that somehow clever process can wish away fundamental inequalities of power and resources.

The third set of tensions that are faced by local governance partnerships are those created by the different expectations of different parts of government at the centre. Most partnerships struggle to balance the demands placed on them by the centre with their own priorities and needs. Each government department is accustomed to a different relationship with their frontline agencies –

some are used to command and control, while others are far more likely to rely on persuasion and the funding of pilot projects. In discussions of performance management systems, therefore, each department tends to expect to replicate its relationship with the whole partnership – leading to very different expectations, which are not always worked through. Partnership working creates as many challenges at the centre as it does within a locality.

Is leadership the answer?

Faced with the confusion caused by all these pressures – much attention has been focused on the need for leadership. And while leadership is crucial if governance partnerships are to work effectively, we need to recognise what good leaders need to be able to do. As Jim Collins pointed out in *Good to Great*:

> *Every time we attribute everything to leadership we are no different from the people in the 1500s who attributed everything they didn't understand (such as famine and plague) to God.*[3]

Currently, there is a tendency for partnerships to be 'underled' – ie despite having, within the partnership, many very senior people with proven leadership capability in their own fields, there is sometimes an absence of collective leadership. This might be because leadership was being 'left up to the council' or because others were playing defensive or opportunistic roles. A decision to exercise leadership commits an individual leader to spend their time and energy, and when they are uncertain about the added value of the partnership, they often attend with a 'watching brief' trying to gauge the importance of this work for their own agendas, but for the time being, withholding the leadership effort that might be needed to offer challenge or propose action.

Leadership within an LSP is in part a decision by individuals or organisations about whether or not to invest their leadership in an LSP, which in turn is based on a judgement about external factors or conditions for success. Since the leadership resources of an organisation are scarce, and cannot be deployed everywhere at once, individuals are choosing how to deploy their leaders and their leadership. The local authority is in a different position, because of the expectations of a community leadership role, and local authorities often work hard to provide leadership at a number of levels. This can sometimes mean that other organisations relax and withdraw still further, confident that leadership is provided. They may then feel disengaged and less driven to provide resources and energy themselves.

As Chesterman and Horne argue,[4] however, there is a danger that a focus on individual leadership competencies draws attention away from developing the 'capacity of networked relationships'. They suggest that 'developing the capacity for local leadership' involves establishing the conditions in which 'solutions are negotiated, not imposed'.

The problems faced by partnerships are not simply to do with poor organisation or lack of focus, they are problems thrown up by the nature of the endeavour. Good leaders will have to find ways to resolve new problems, through new sorts of solutions.

Partnerships are an example of 'leadership systems' and need not simply be about leadership from several parts of the system – from politicians, for example, from the leaders of key public agencies, and from leaders in the community – but a leadership process that can sustain the health of the system as a whole. A key leadership role is often that of constructing both the authority and power to act, connecting partnership decisions both to the wider community and to the delivery capability of different partner agencies. It is as important to maintain relationships through the informal spaces between meetings as it is to intervene effectively in the meetings themselves – as useful to create processes in which the leadership of others can be encouraged as it is to lead oneself. Building the capacity of the whole system, making it possible for others to invest their leadership, creating space for the discovery of new solutions, being willing to let go of tenaciously held short-term goals in the long-term interests of the whole – all these will be important in developing good leadership systems.

If partnerships are to find the few key areas of critical intervention that can combine the resources of many agencies to make a significant impact on the most important problems, leaders will have to be able to make balancing judgements – and trade-offs – between the many different outcomes wanted in each place. Not everything can be achieved everywhere.

It will require a new sort of local politics that is less adversarial and more investigative – based on dialogue and negotiation. It will require new sorts of managers within local authorities, health authorities, police authorities, quangos etc – capable of thinking about the 'whole system' and making balancing judgements. But alongside this, new thinking will be needed both from civil servants and from ministers – using systems thinking to intervene only when it helps, recognising the trade-offs that have to be made at local level when resources are shrinking and accepting that demands for short-term activities and excessive paperwork simply distracts attention and wastes resource that could be used to achieve long-term goals.

Some partnerships do seem to be on the brink of a breakthrough. We are also, now, seeing communities beginning to work collaboratively; already there are fascinating examples of communities under stress – particularly because of reactions to the Muslim community or the threat of terrorism – coming together in sophisticated dialogue brokered by the local authority. It is perhaps more difficult to find prefiguring examples of change at the centre, but even here, however, there are hopeful signs. Government offices of the regions are equipping themselves to work on a multidisciplinary basis across government departments and understand the big picture in each city, county and region, and civil servants and ministers are beginning to work together to understand the impact that all their different interventions make on a single area.

There is scope to take collaborative working far further – to reconfigure services radically across boundaries to generate new sorts of provision. In the private sector, there is now talk of 'chaordic' organisations, which are primarily networks operating with fluid delivery but strong governance. These sorts of models are even more likely to be needed in the public sector. The next challenge is to design approaches to governance that can secure strong legitimacy and accountability in modern, transparent interactive terms for networks of organisations that are fluid and creative. We need a debate to enable us to understand the systems and processes that work fast and well for networked organisations – one that involves the media and the public, since they will also have to learn to relate differently to a collaborative state. Attention will need to be paid to the leadership processes that build relationships of trust and reciprocity – not simply at locality level but between localities, regions and the centre.

Finally, we have to break out of the 'chicken and egg' problem we currently face: until partnership working is proved effective people on all sides are reluctant to commit; the idea of allowing experimentation without positive proof that targets will be achieved generates nervousness; under pressure organisations default to tried and tested organisational silos. We need therefore to be ambitiously realistic, recognise the constraints on all sides, and do sensible things that can build confidence as we learn to 'let go'. Collaborative working will become effective only if confidence can be generated in the ability to deliver in new ways. Perhaps the most important leadership role, right now, is to help to contain the anxiety generated during the journey.

Sue Goss is principal of national, regional and local services at the Office of Public Management

Notes

1   Communities and Local Government, *Strong and Prosperous Communities: The local government white paper* (Norwich: TSO, 2006), available at www.communities.gov.uk/index.asp?id=1503999 (accessed 12 Mar 2007).
2   See Lyons Inquiry, *National Prosperity, Local Choice and Civic Engagement* (London: HMSO, 2006).
3   J Collins, *Good to Great* (New York: Random House Business Books, Oct 2001).
4   D Chesterman and M Horne, *Local Authority* (London: Demos, 2002).

3. Roots of cooperation and routes to collaboration

Barry Quirk

The drive to encourage collaborative work in local government stems from the disappointments of the 'New Public Management'. For a while in the 1980s and early 1990s, it was thought that focused single-purpose public sector agencies that adopted best private sector practice would most probably deliver more effective outcomes. However, this approach flew in the face of the developments in social planning, which had increasingly identified the interconnected nature of social problems (the so-called 'wicked problems'[1]) and the need to adopt shared solutions across organisational boundaries to help solve these problems.

In the early 1990s a new stream of public management thinking developed in the USA around the two ideas of public agency collaboration and the production of public value. In 1992, John Bryson and Barbara Crosby published perhaps the seminal text on collaborative working in the public sector. In the introduction to their book, *Leadership for the Common Good*, they wrote:

> *We live in a world where no one is 'in charge'. No one organisation or institution has the legitimacy, power, authority, or intelligence to act alone on important public issues and still make substantial headway against the problems that threaten us all. . . . Many organisations or institutions are involved, affected or have a partial responsibility to act, and the information*

necessary to address public issues is incomplete and unevenly distributed among the involved organisations. As a result, we live in a 'shared power' world, a world in which organisations and institutions must share objectives, activities, resources, power or authority in order to achieve collective gains or minimise losses.[2]

In the UK the response to shortcomings of the New Public Management paradigm used slightly different language. The debate focused more on how the incoming Labour government in 1997 could reform public services by a mix of investment and centrally driven performance targets. This resulted in a pluralistic approach that attempted to encourage New Public Management approaches where they were thought to be needed and networked,[3] joined up or holistic[4] where these made more sense.

A decade later, there is a widespread recognition that centrally driven targets have been overplayed and that public institutions need to be more responsive to customers and citizens. The UK government's approach to public service reform continues to place emphasis on centrally determined targets, competition and choice but it also gives fresh encouragement to 'bottom-up' collaboration.[5] The development of 'Local Area Agreements' – formal multi-agency agreements in local government areas to share goals such as reducing crime and improving health – has provided additional impetus to strategic collaboration at the local level.

Now with the review of local government's future by Sir Michael Lyons,[6] there is a formal recognition that the purposes of local government extend beyond being a service delivery agent for Whitehall. Councils are being encouraged by Lyons to become positive agents of collaboration – shaping places, convening public services and enabling citizens to come together to exercise choice about their future.

Collaboration to expand public value can already be found in a rich stream of practice at the local level. And the best of local government is at the centre of collaborative effort – linking communities together, forging alliances between local businesses, between local public agencies as well as convening public service strategies locally. But collaboration is not simply a tool of strategic management. It is a style of thinking and acting at the level of practice and operation. This does not come easily.

Collaboration and the cooperative spirit

In a world of action and achievement, cooperative working is often seen as an 'unnatural' activity for management – the antithesis of getting things done. Principles of market-driven efficiency have been internalised by many agencies, with the implication that competitive self-interest fuels innovation and progress and that, in consequence, single-purpose teams or organisations that focus their energies on achieving singular purposes are the most likely to succeed. According to this way of thinking, working in partnership with others may be necessary from time to time, but things get done when tasks are simple and separate. In a world that prefers 'do-it-yourself', cooperation becomes a spirit to avoid not a spirit to embrace.

In several policy areas the UK government has introduced legislation that requires public bodies to 'cooperate' with others. In tackling crime and disorder several public bodies have a duty to cooperate with police authorities and local government – on whom prime responsibilities for public action are placed. And in the area of children's services and safeguarding children, again, some agencies are required to cooperate with local government. In both cases the imposition of these 'duties to cooperate' have been relatively successful – so much so that last year's local government white paper extended the duty to other agencies (schools and GPs, for example).[7]

However, something that was thought to be an emergent and organic act – cooperation – has become something planned and engineered by the state. The very act of legislating for cooperation in these areas perhaps indicates not just the complexity of the issues concerned but also the strength of the forces that counter cooperation.

Why are people so attracted to doing things themselves rather than working with others in a team endeavour? Perhaps there is some ancient barrier in our psychology to working in a cooperative way. Perhaps the second meaning of the word 'collaboration' – acting treasonably with the enemy – helps explain the inner problem. If I cooperate with you at work rather than someone else, I have changed the focus of my fidelity in my working life.

Maybe managers are naturally driven to dividing tasks and labour according to specialism and 'cooperation' is a word which, on face value, implies discussion and compromise rather than active execution. With all this lexical baggage it is hardly surprising that collaborative work is hard going. Some people seem dead set against it from the outset.

If we are to be convinced of the benefits of collaboration perhaps we need to demonstrate that cooperation is natural, runs with the grain of social and economic life, and is central to a democratic society. We need to overcome the thinking that cooperation is an unnatural activity that is attempting to reverse the realities of competitive self-interest that make open-market societies flourish. Thus to follow collaborative routes it may be necessary to have an appreciation of its roots in theory. What are the sources of cooperative effort given the apparently all-pervasive competitive individualism in human nature, in society, in the economy and in the political sphere?

In fact, the lessons and advantages of interpersonal cooperation have been identified in a range of disciplines and fields of enquiry. In particular, the lessons that have been learnt in the distinctly separate spheres of biology, economics (both influenced strongly by 'game theory') and political philosophy are cogent and strikingly relevant. They all demonstrate that cooperation is not only possible, but also in many senses quite natural.

The cooperative gene

In biology, significant developments in evolutionary theory over the past 50 years have recast the understanding of how animals success-fully evolved. The existence of widespread cooperative behaviour between animals – across species or within species – was witnessed for many hundreds of years but never really understood. But the sheer extent and degree of cooperation between animals seemed to fly in the face of the supposed 'tooth and claw' survival instinct.

Therefore, cooperative behaviour in animals, enacted without the benefit of (human) conscious intention, is not now seen as somehow anomalous to a dominant pattern of selfish behaviour and instinct but rather as a central feature of species' successful evolutionary strategy.

Of course, this may have little bearing on human evolutionary development where cooperative behaviour arose first through conscious and intentional 'group selection' mechanisms;[8] and then second, through the relatively more recent development of intergenerational cultural pressures of custom and tradition blended alongside the march of technological progress and the ever extending intellectual reach of reason. Nonetheless, it can be said that in a very real sense cooperation has its deepest roots in genes.

Cooperate to win

In economics, ideas about cooperation have their roots in arguments about the benefits of market exchange and specialisation as well as, again, in game theory. The Nobel prize-winning economist Kenneth Arrow expressed the first of these arguments simply and elegantly:

> *First, individuals are different and have different talents; and second, individuals' efficiency in the performance of social tasks usually improves with specialisation. We need cooperation to achieve specialisation of function. This involves all the elements of trade and the division of labour. The blacksmith in the primitive village is not expected to eat horseshoes; he specialises in making horseshoes, the farmer supplies him with grain in exchange, and both (this is the critical point) can be made better off.*[9]

Of course, this form of cooperation is spontaneous in character and emerges from market exchange rather than from some form of central or strategic plan. But in the economy, cooperation arises both within and across businesses. Companies develop management strategies to encourage cooperation internally while also adopting management strategies to collaborate with other companies for mutual benefit. Indeed, the development of market economies, based on successful companies that produced substantial wealth and value, is predicated on staggering degrees of voluntary cooperation between people working within these companies over extended periods of their working lives.[10]

Once again, collaboration in the real world appears to contradict the theory. There is a school of classical economics that argues that collaboration is in some ways unnatural – that rational individuals slavishly pursue their own short-term self-interest even when collaboration might deliver a better outcome. This is sometimes illustrated through the 'prisoners' dilemma', where two prisoners are incapable of cooperating for mutual benefit.

However, Robert Axelrod's famous examination of the results of many thousands of games of 'the prisoner's dilemma' found that, in repeated games, cooperation was actually the most successful strategy.[11] This led him to conclude that the basis for cooperation lay in the existence of stable and durable relationships (where reciprocity could flourish). Of course, in government, most 'games' are repeated. Certain circumstances, he argued, help cooperation emerge:

1 'Enlarge the shadow of the future' – mutual cooperation is stable if the future is sufficiently important relative to the present.
2 Change the 'payoffs' so that non-cooperation is more heavily penalised.
3 Teach people to care about the welfare of others.
4 Teach people about the benefits of reciprocity.
6 Improve people's abilities to recognise the pattern of other people's responses so as to sustain long-run cooperation.

Other theorists argue that cooperation is more likely to occur where groups are small, which increases the visibility and predictability of individual's actions (increasing size would diminish the willingness of team members to contribute their discretionary effort) and where rules of engagement and sanctions are clear and accepted.[12]

But the evidence is that ever larger teams and companies have survived and thrived in the global economy. Moreover, there are very many related management strategies that encourage cooperation between companies. These collaborative strategies fall short of conventional mergers or acquisitions. But they include alliances between companies in complementary sectors, horizontal alliances between companies with different specialisms or complementary resources operating within broadly similar sectors, and involve various companies in ever deeper vertical supply chains within the same sector. In addition there are several companies, particularly those within the consultancy and outsourcing sectors, that specialise in collaboration and that market themselves as collaborative experts.[13]

Traditionally, most inter-company collaborations involve setting up and managing joint ventures. But the past two decades in the UK corporate sector has witnessed the growth of 'strategic alliances' which, compared with joint ventures, are characterised by the following:

O They have greater uncertainty and ambiguity.
O Value is created and captured by partners in more
    emergent ways.
O The relationship is harder to predict.
O Today's ally may be tomorrow's rival.
O Managing the relationship over time is more important
    than the partnership's formal design.
O Success depends on the ability to adapt to changing
    circumstances.[14]

Those business commentators who have focused more specifically on how companies develop their capacity to collaborate have discovered that it centres on companies' desire for partnership, the ease of coordination across activities and services and the capability of management to partner across organisations.[15]

Corporate alliances hold the prospect of increased profits or decreased costs for companies but they also contain potential pitfalls. Any formal collaborative effort (where, say, budgets are pooled and strategies conjoined) requires considerable forethought and planning. Basic financial foundations need to be agreed and in place, while legal issues need to be thoroughly worked through in considerable detail.

It is very common for these foundational finance and legal issues to dominate concerns about collaboration between companies. Fears of cost-shunting or unfair burden-sharing crowd into this aspect of the agenda.

However, very few collaborative efforts fail because of poor financial and legal frameworks. Many more fail because insufficient effort has been paid to aligning management strategies. More fundamentally, failures due to strategy misalignments are themselves dwarfed by the number that fail because relationships between key principals fail or become damaged over time.

From 'favours beget favours' to promoting cooperation

Within political philosophy, concepts of cooperation have lengthy, complex and interwoven roots in moral teachings and in political theory. For some, cooperation was seen to arise freely from people exercising their rights and freedoms to associate with each other in common cause. For others, cooperation was seen to be more evident in the working of the state – marshalling collective action in the context of society's broader competitive individualism.

The moral aspect of cooperation is best illustrated through the famous 'golden rule' that finds expression in all the great world religions and which has been deeply influential for many centuries among people of very diverse cultures. The golden rule is best interpreted as saying: 'Treat others only in ways that you are willing to be treated if you find yourself in exactly the same situation.' It can be said to underscore a moral approach to reciprocity which governs social life and lubricates cooperative endeavour.

Despite its resonance with much religious teaching, the golden rule's cooperative sentiments may not be fuelled by compassion and sympathy but instead reflect a restricted reciprocity based on a 'favours begets favours' approach. This was perhaps best outlined by David Hume in his 1739 *Treatise on Human Nature* when he wrote:

> *I learn to do service to another, without bearing him any real kindness, because I forsee that he will return my service in expectation of another of the same kind, and in order to maintain the same correspondence of good offices with me and others. And accordingly, after I have served him and he is in possession of the advantages arising from my action, he is induced to perform his part, forseeing the consequence of his refusal.*[16]

But political philosophy is arguably less concerned with the degree of cooperative behaviour between citizens and more with the role of the state in respect of its citizenry. And at its simplest, the state's role has grown commensurate with the growth of the rule of law (regulating and enforcing promises to cooperate) and growing complexity in the protection of liberty and free association.

The liberal philosopher John Rawls argues that a core function of public officials (whether elected or appointed) in an open democratic society is the promotion of public reason. In a representative democracy citizens vote for representatives and not for particular laws. Therefore those elected (or appointed) need to explain how they exercised justice in the performance of their duties. And he says that they need to do so within a 'criterion of reciprocity'. By this he means: 'When terms are proposed as the most reasonable terms of fair cooperation, those proposing them must think it at least reasonable for others to accept them, as free and equal citizens, and not as dominated or manipulated or under pressure caused by inferior political or social position.'[17]

Thus according to Rawls a key feature of the purposes of public institutions – and hence the purposes of those elected and appointed to serve the public – is the promotion of civility and the fostering of cooperation between people. In short, cooperation underscores the very essence of public purposes in democratic societies.

Cooperation is therefore not an 'unnatural activity'. It has real roots in genes and in evolution itself; it has roots in the background fabric of trust and reciprocity which enables the market economy to flourish; and it has roots at the very centre of how liberal democratic governments function.

Local collaboration

People cooperate with people they know, with people whom they meet. Perhaps it is not surprising then that the site of most cooperation is local. And perhaps it is not surprising that the source of most collaborative effort between organisations is found at the local level.

In each and every locality people are working within and across organisations for collaborative advantage. It is plainly the case that public agencies can increase their effectiveness and efficiency through better collaboration. But two other aspects are equally clear.

First, that collaborative approaches can be used by public agencies in their work of building value with their customers (through co-production).

Second, councils can use collaborative approaches in their work with citizens – through the promotion of civicism and cooperation among their citizens generally. After all, the highest purpose of local government is to enable its communities to live together in harmony and peace. As such, the tools of alliance and coalition building and the techniques of establishing consent while enabling dissent are as relevant to the sphere of politics and community as they are to the sphere of management and organisation.

A three-dimensional approach to collaboration at the local level is as follows:

1   Collaborating within an organisation:
     o   collaborative working within any team focused on
          achieving any common objective (say, street wardens
          in a town centre attempting to reduce crime and
          anti-social behaviour)

     ○   collaborative working across different functional teams to achieve any common objective (say, all employers from different professional disciplines and operational areas seeking to improve the quality of experience in a town centre).

2   Collaborating between organisations:
     ○   collaborative operational working between like organisations in the same locality doing similar things but with slightly different capabilities (such as is found in school collaborations on curricula, facilities and management overheads and in collaborations that can be seen across GPs surgeries)
     ○   teams from two or more different public agencies operationally focused on achieving any common objective (say, education and social care professionals, probation officers, police officers and public health officials attempting to reduce risks to children)
     ○   strategic agreements between public agencies to align their goals, strategies and resources to achieve commonly agreed purposes (such as section 31 agreements between local government and the health service in respect of services for people with mental health problems).

3   Collaboration with the community:
     ○   collaborative working between groups of citizens and local agencies to design and/or deliver local public services for community benefit (such as occurs with some community groups running leisure facilities for wider public benefit and usage)
     ○   collaborative work between citizens or communities that generates public value and which improves public life in an area (such as with neighbourhood watch schemes or with interfaith groups that seek to generate inter-community liaison and dialogue).

In this three-fold approach collaboration is less a management strategy and more a way of thinking and acting. If the local state was more collaborative by pursuing simply the first two dimensions, councils would focus more on achieving public objectives through better team working and through sharing goals, strategies, resources and priorities with others.

This might make them more able to enhance public goods and services in their localities and their customers might be more satisfied – but agency does not stop at the door of the state. Citizens need to be collaboratively engaged with public agencies or else the collaborative state could simply promote passivity.

From this perspective our approach to collaboration should be wide and not narrow. Yes, there are substantial benefits to be gained in collaboration across public organisations – to build public value as well as to reduce costs. But the management agenda of sharing service costs, aggregating demand and supply and reducing overheads does not describe the totality of the possible. A wider civic purpose pervades democratic local government. Councils will attain the position marked out for them in the Lyons report only if they collaborate in 360 degrees – with their citizens, with local businesses, with suppliers and service partners, and with their own staff.

Councils should adopt a collaborative approach not because it enables their objectives to be more readily delivered, but because it is more likely to widen their horizons beyond their own narrow institutional imperatives and encourage more cooperative and more civil approaches among local citizens.

Barry Quirk is chief executive of the London Borough of Lewisham.

Notes

1   The term 'wicked issues' or 'wicked problems' has been used for several years – its uses stem from an academic paper by H Rittel and M Webber, 'Dilemmas in a general theory of planning', *Policy Sciences* 4 (1973).

2   J Bryson and B Crosby, *Leadership for the Common Good: Tackling problems in a shared-power world* (San Francisco: Jossey-Bass, 1992).

3   W Kickert et al, *Managing Complex Networks: Strategies for the public sector* (London: Sage, 1997).
4   Perri 6 et al, *Governing in the Round: Strategies for holistic government* (London: Demos, 1999).
5   Prime Minister's Strategy Unit, *The UK Government's Approach to Public Service Reform: A discussion paper* (London: HMSO, 2006).
6   Lyons Inquiry, *National Prosperity, Local Choice and Civic Engagement* (London: HMSO, 2006).
7   Communities and Local Government, *Strong and Prosperous Communities: The local government white paper* (Norwich: TSO, 2006), available at www.communities.gov.uk/index.asp?id=1503999 (accessed 12 Mar 2007).
8   E Sober and D Wilson, 'Unto others: the evolution and psychology of unselfish behaviour', in LD Katz (ed), *Evolutionary Origins of Morality: Cross-disciplinary perspectives* (Thorverton, UK: Imprint Academic, 2000).
9   K Arrow, *The Limits of Organisation* (New York: Norton, 1974).
10   P Seabright, *The Company of Strangers: A natural history of economic life* (Princeton, NJ: Princeton University Press, 2004).
11   R Axelrod, *The Evolution of Cooperation* (New York: Basic Books, 1984).
12   For information about pressure groups in US politics see, for example, M Olson, *The Logic of Collective Action* (Cambridge, MA: Harvard University Press, 1965).
13   For an example of a company marketing itself as a collaborative exemplar see www.capgemini.com/collaboration (accessed 10 Mar 2007).
14   YL Doz and G Hamel, *Alliance Advantage* (Boston: Harvard Business Press, 1998).
15   D Lambert and M Knemeyer, 'We're in this together', *Harvard Business Review*, Dec 2004.
16   D Hume, *A Treatise of Human Nature: Being an attempt to introduce the experimental method of reasoning into moral subjects* (first published anonymously in 1739), available at http://etext.library.adelaide.edu.au/h/hume/david/h92t/ (accessed 12 Mar 2007).
17   J Rawls, *The Law of Peoples* (Oxford: Oxford University Press, 1999).

4. The conditions for collaboration

Early learning from Wales
Steve Martin and Adrian Webb

The Welsh model of the collaborative state

England and Wales have similar histories, legal frameworks, performance regimes, resources and levels of social need. Public service providers in the two countries therefore face the same strategic challenges. Personal tax thresholds are low by European standards and as a result there is pressure for increased efficiency. Rapidly expanding choice in the private consumer goods market is fuelling rising public expectations of service quality. Technological advances (particularly in medicine) and an ageing population are driving up the costs of welfare provision. As has been well documented elsewhere,[1] the combined impact of these forces has been to lay waste traditional notions of the welfare state. Standardised services delivered by state organisations operating through command and control mechanisms are no longer thought to be up to the job. The public is said to demand more efficient and more personalised services tailored to individual needs and preferences, and available 24/7.

The big question is: how best to achieve the transformation in public services that is required to meet these changing needs and expectations? Intriguingly, in spite of the similarities in the contexts in which they are operating and a shared view that public services do need to be reformed, policy-makers in England and Wales are in the process of developing quite different answers to this challenge. England has focused on markets, modernisation and, latterly, on cost control. By contrast, Wales has chosen to reform its public services by relying entirely on the principle of greater collaboration between different organisations – a path which requires a comprehensive overhaul of the country's entire governance system.

Policy-makers in Wales have been less enthusiastic about externally imposed performance management frameworks, targets and plans, and have rejected league tables and notions of 'earned autonomy' altogether. They claim that, in a relatively small country, audit and inspection are less important. With just 22 local councils, 14 NHS trusts, four police forces and three fire brigades, ministers and civil servants can meet regularly with all of the chief executives, council leaders, chairs of trusts, chief constables and chief fire officers.

And in this close-knit policy community it is, they claim, unnecessary to 'name and shame' poor performers because pressure can be exerted behind the scenes.

As in England, there is interest in securing efficiency savings, but there is no real appetite for reducing the scale of the state. Indeed, as part of its much vaunted 'bonfire of the quangos', the Welsh Assembly Government has recently re-absorbed the staff and functions of three of the largest arm's length Assembly-sponsored public bodies – the Welsh Development Agency, Education and Learning Wales, and the Welsh Tourist Board.

Above all, though, Wales has eschewed market solutions centred on competition between service providers and increased choice for service users. In *Making the Connections*,[2] a key policy statement published in 2004, the Welsh Assembly Government argued that consumer choice in public services was inappropriate and unworkable in Wales because population densities in most parts of the country are too low to support a multiplicity of providers. Moreover, it suggested, people do not want to be treated simply as consumers of services. They are citizens who wish to express their needs and preferences primarily through 'voice' (public participation) rather than market-based choice. They want equality of outcomes as well as opportunity,[3] and set great store by 'joined-up' services. *Making the Connections* argued that the best route to more efficient and effective public services in Wales was not therefore competition but collaboration – both vertical (between local and central government) and horizontal (between local authorities, between councils and other local public agencies, and between the public, private and voluntary sectors).

The limits of consumer choice

This collaborative model is the most important manifestation of what the Welsh first minister describes as the 'clear red water' which has opened up between Cardiff and Westminster. It reflects both the 'communitaire' tradition in Welsh culture and a profound distrust of the consumer choice model. And there are indeed good grounds for questioning claims made for public services reform via competition and individual (as opposed to collective) consumer choice.

Welsh geography and demography does, as the Assembly government claims, make it difficult to create markets for all services, especially in sparsely populated areas. The Welsh public is undoubtedly unwilling (and in some cases unable) to travel large distances for primary education and routine health care, for example, and genuine choice may therefore be an unrealistic expectation outside of large metropolitan areas (which Wales clearly lacks).

Second, consumer choice can drive efficiency only if service users act on accurate perceptions of their own needs, of competing products, of price and of the available budget. None of these conditions readily apply in the case of most public services. Users frequently have very little appreciation of the cost of the services they receive. As recent debates about the availability of new cancer drugs illustrate, most users demand the most effective interventions regardless of the cost to the public purse or the opportunity cost. Furthermore, competition can drive efficiency in 'markets' for 'free' goods only where there is excess production and the political will to close down less successful providers. Neither of these conditions exists in the case of most public services, especially those for vulnerable users. Individual consumer choices cannot therefore promote efficiency – even in theory – and in practice they may actually lead to inefficiencies.

Third, the choice and competition model assumes that consumers have equal ability to make effective choices. This is also untrue. In practice the best informed and most articulate will be able to make the best procurement choices. Less well-informed users, who are often the most vulnerable, often lose out, and choice can therefore lead to inequality. Moreover, even well-informed and normally confident service users may find it difficult to make rational decisions at times of acute stress, such as serious illness or sudden bereavement, when they are most in need of a range of public services.

Fourth, there is no evidence to suggest that users value a plurality of providers per se. If monopoly suppliers can personalise services in order to meet individual needs and preferences most members of the public are likely to be content with them. Indeed, research suggests that many people feel ill equipped to make choices between providers and would prefer not to have to do so.[4]

Fifth, there is evidence that the notion of 'customers' or 'consumers' of public services may have a corrosive effect on public perceptions of service providers. As Taylor-Gooby argues,[5] the public can become more satisfied consumers of public services while losing confidence in the institutions that provide them. And recent research concludes that this is precisely what has happened in the case of English local government in recent years – there has been a steady improvement in most local services provided but surveys show declining satisfaction with the overall performance of local councils.[6]

Making the collaborative model a reality

Doubts about the capacity of consumer choice to drive public service improvement do not of course mean that an alternative 'collaborative approach', such as that espoused by policy-makers in Wales, will necessarily fare any better. In theory, collaboration within and between public services is often an entirely rational way to proceed, but in practice it frequently proves elusive. As in England, there is a plethora of partnerships in Wales, many of which are perceived to be resource intensive and ineffective.[7] The difficulties of partnership working are well known.[8] Public services share a common goal of enhancing the public good, but in reality the bureaucratic 'silos' that characterise government encourage the pursuit of more narrowly focused goals defined by the responsibilities of particular professions, organisations or departments.

As a result, significant and sustained collaboration is unlikely to arise voluntarily. It is naïve to rely on 'goodwill' and 'unselfish' behaviour. Collaboration is an inherently time-consuming and uncertain activity, and governments must therefore incentivise it by either imposing stiff penalties for non-collaborative behaviour and/or by offering substantial rewards to agencies that do choose to work together. In particular they have to create a climate in which service providers have strong incentives to pool resources, accountability and sovereignty. Funding mechanisms must therefore facilitate joint accountability for jointly owned resources applied to shared outcomes.

For their part, service providers need to know how to negotiate win–win outcomes. This requires the careful cultivation of a 'bargaining culture' and of tough negotiating skills.

All of this implies the need for a significant departure from the existing machinery, culture and working practices of central and local government. And the key question for policy-makers in Wales is whether, having committed themselves so firmly to a collaborative model of public services reform, they can create the governance system capable of delivering it.

A recent independent review under the chairmanship of Sir Jeremy Beecham, published in July 2006,[9] concluded that the current performance of public services in Wales was patchy and lagged behind that in comparable areas of England in a number of important respects. In particular, although Wales spends more per capita on health, both hospital waiting time and ambulance response times are significantly longer than in England.[10]

The report nevertheless endorsed the Welsh Assembly Government's overall strategy. Rejecting calls for a comprehensive re-organisation of local government, it argued that public services reform in Wales could indeed be achieved through much greater collaboration among providers.

But it argued that reforms designed to foster collaboration need to go much further and faster if the Welsh model is to succeed. NHS trusts, police forces, ambulance services, councils and others should combine 'back office' functions in order to reap economies of scale. A far more mixed economy of provision has to be created. And there has to be a move away from the Welsh tradition of public sector provision towards a public services philosophy based on 'managed networks', which use the power of public funding to create partnerships between the private, public and voluntary sectors.

Above all, however, the report argued for a more determined, and different, approach to collaboration. It said that schools and colleges serving rural populations must stop competing for students and instead work together in order to ensure that they can provide a full post-16 curriculum. Neighbouring local authorities should pool budgets and make much more use of joint appointments in order to create the critical mass needed to sustain investment in new technologies and avoid counterproductive competition for top managerial talent and other skills that are in short supply (such as experienced social workers). And, the report concludes, the Assembly Government and the National Assembly need to re-engineer 'silo-based' internal administrative systems, funding streams, planning regimes and approaches to scrutiny in order to make effective partnership between providers possible.

The report endorsed the combination of pooled sovereignty and bargaining/negotiation approaches to sustainable collaboration that we have outlined above. But it acknowledged that this presents huge challenges for national and local government and requires a comprehensive overhaul of the entire governance system. Non-devolved functions, such as policing and the benefits systems, which are driven by priorities set in Westminster and Whitehall that may not be compatible with the needs of Wales, present a particular challenge. However, the National Assembly for Wales and the Welsh Assembly Government have to accept primary responsibility for ensuring and facilitating effective collaboration at local level.

The Beecham review team identified three principal barriers to the fundamental reforms that it believes are required: the complexity of the governance system; the capacity for effective collaborative working; and the existing culture of many public services.

Complexity

While the Welsh Assembly Government is comparatively compact and in theory ought therefore to have the ability readily to bridge internal boundaries, the reality is not dissimilar to that in most major government bureaucracies. Substantially discrete blocks of policies are managed within departmental 'silos' and according to a model of government – inherited from Whitehall – which pays only limited attention to the delivery of integrated outcomes on the ground. This is despite an early, very public and undoubtedly sincere commitment by the Welsh Assembly Government to achieving more 'joined-up government'. The result is sector-based business processes with different planning cycles, performance frameworks, funding regimes and legislative requirements. Buttressed by deeply entrenched professional and sectoral boundaries, these are extremely difficult to break free from.

Policy-makers in Wales pride themselves on the co-terminosity of local authorities and local health boards, and this has indeed helped to promote joint action in primary health. But there is a much more variable geometry in other policy areas including, for example, the six Spatial Plan areas, four regional transport consortia, four police forces, three fire brigades and three health 'regions'. Moreover, while there is an agreement in principle between the Assembly Government and the Welsh Local Government Association that local government services should be funded through non-hypothecated grant to allow maximum flexibility at local level, there are in fact more than 60 specific revenue and capital grant schemes that emanate from different parts of the Assembly Government, each of which has its own guidance, objectives, bidding timetables and monitoring requirements.

This complexity is mirrored in other sectors and across sectors –

local government, the police, fire and the NHS are subject to almost entirely separate performance management frameworks and, as in England, there are multiple inspectorates including in local government alone the Wales Audit Office, the Social Services Inspectorate Wales, the Care Standards Inspectorate Wales and Estyn.

Capacity

The Beecham review concluded that a second obstacle to the success of the collaborative model is that existing managerial capacity is spread far too thinly. It argued that Wales needs rapidly to develop a new cadre of leaders and managers who are able to operate successfully across sectors. There is also an acute shortage of people with skills in project management, asset management, workforce planning and, crucially, the approaches to commissioning that are required to create and manage networks of providers.

Culture

The report concludes that the existing culture of public services militates against collaboration. Current structures and processes engender a culture of compliance that promotes uniformity and consistency but stifles innovation and flexibility. The Assembly Government sees its role as being primarily concerned with framing policy; it has not in the past taken responsibility for ensuring effective delivery 'on the ground'. Performance frameworks are not designed to foster and reward well-managed service providers.

Wales lacks a systematic approach to identifying good practice or promoting inter-organisational learning – within and between sectors. There is resistance to working with the private and voluntary sectors. Scrutiny – both in the National Assembly and at local level – is too often focused on processes rather than outcomes and rarely takes a 'cross-cutting' approach. Crucially, policy-makers in Wales have been averse to performance comparisons – between organisations and between areas. There are, for example, no equivalents of star ratings or CPA (comprehensive performance assessment) scores in Wales. Nor, in spite of the importance that policy-makers in Wales claim to attach to citizen-centred governance, are there robust data on public satisfaction. The Beecham report saw a strong commitment to benchmarking performance against appropriate comparators, combined with far greater public engagement, a far better informed citizenry and a much more mature public debate about policy options, as important prerequisites of the creation of the collaborative state.

Conclusion

The 'collaborative state' is not then a soft option. For it to become a reality there will need to be a fundamental change in central government's role – away from a preoccupation with policy formulation and reliance on arm's length command and control towards a much greater focus on delivery and 'engaged leadership' of managed networks of service providers. Local agencies will need to be much more willing to work together. Central and local government will have to develop mechanisms for pooling resources and accountability in respect of key outcomes.

Wales is still a long way off offering a working model of this collaborative state. At present, the level of partnership working and the successes and failures look very similar to those on display in England. But it does offer a distinctive vision for the future of public services that is remarkable for the way in which it apparently eschews almost all other drivers of improvement in favour of a single-minded reliance on collaboration. At this very early stage – just two years after the publication of the outline strategy – it is impossible to say whether this bold strategy will produce more efficient, joined-up and responsive public services that are fit for the twenty-first century.

However, because of its similarities and proximity to England, Wales does provide a fascinating 'natural laboratory' in which to test out the potential of an alternative (and now increasingly coherent) vision of the collaborative state. The Welsh model faces considerable challenges, and may fall flat on its face. Alternatively, if the kinds of measures that the Beecham report advocates are adopted, it could come to be seen as an exemplar of small-country governance which offers a route to transformed public services which is of interest even to its much larger neighbour. Either way, for policy-makers and academic commentators, the Welsh approach is one to watch.

Steve Martin is director of the Local & Regional Government Research Unit, Cardiff University and chair of Pontypridd & Rhondda NHS Trust. Adrian Webb is non-executive director of the Welsh Assembly Government Executive Board.

Notes

1   See for example J Clarke and J Newman, *The Managerial State* (London: Sage, 2005).

2   Welsh Assembly Government, *Making the Connections: Delivering better services for Wales* (Cardiff: Welsh Assembly Government, 2004), available at: http://new.wales.gov.uk/about/strategy/makingtheconnections (accessed 10 Mar 2007).

3   M Drayford, 'Wales and a third term of New Labour: devolution and the development of difference', *Critical Social Policy* 25, no 4 (2005).

4   See, for example, BMG Research, *Qualitative Development for the Annual Survey of Local Government and its Services: Objective A*, report to the Office of the Deputy Prime Minister (London: ODPM, 2004); and C Needham, 'Consultation a cure for local government', *Parliamentary Affairs* 55, no 4 (2002).

5   P Taylor-Gooby, 'The efficiency/trust dilemma', *Health, Risk and Society* 8, no 2 (2006).

6   S Martin and T Bovaird, *Meta-evaluation of the Local Government Modernisation Agenda: Progress report on service improvement in local government* (London: ODPM, 2005), available at: www.communities.gov.uk/index.asp?id=1162421 (accessed 8 Mar 2007).

7   G Bristow et al, *Partnership Working Between the Public, Private and Voluntary Sectors in Wales* (Cardiff: Welsh Assembly Government, 2003), available at www.clrgr.cf.ac.uk/research/wagpartnerships.html (accessed 8 Mar 2007).

8   A Webb, 'Coordination: a problem in public sector management', *Policy and Politics* 19, no 4 (1991); and Public Services Productivity Panel, *Working Together: Effective partnership working on the ground* (London: HM Treasury, 2002), available at www.idea.gov.uk (accessed 12 Mar 2007).

9   Welsh Assembly Government, *Beyond Boundaries: Citizen-centred local services for Wales* (Cardiff: Welsh Assembly Government, 2006), available at: http://new.wales.gov.uk/about/strategy/makingtheconnections/beechamreview (accessed 8 Mar 2007).

10 Auditor General for Wales, *NHS Waiting Times in Wales* (Cardiff: Wales Audit Office, 2005); see also G Bevan and C Hood, 'Have targets improved performance in the English NHS?', *British Medical Journal* 322, no 7538 (2006).

5. Working together for stronger Victorian communities

Yehudi Blacher and David Adams

The idea of collaboration is now well entrenched in public policy and linked to new ideas around devolution and network governance,[1] yet the actual administrative arrangements necessary to give effect to the idea are still emerging. In this case study we canvass the 'organising' aspects that give administrative form to collaboration. We do this through the lens of the Victorian government's community-strengthening strategy – since to be effective, community strengthening requires substantial collaboration with communities, with other departments and with other sectors. Our view is that the idea of collaboration will become reality only through new forms of governance since our existing forms are built on a historical model that privileges hierarchy over collaboration.

From programmes to people and places

Most Western liberal democratic states reflect versions of West-minster government, which brought with it the public administration arrangements of functionally organised government departments (health, education, justice, agriculture, transport etc) within which the programme format dominates as the business model and output budgeting as the dominant resource allocation mechanism. This three-way division (departments to organise functions, programmes to deliver them and outputs to control resources) guarantees a certain level of efficiency, but does so by making communities invisible to government, and governments opaque and difficult to navigate for communities.

These functionally organised agencies based on Weberian bureaucracy developed a mass production format requiring relatively little co-production or collaboration. A little consultation here and there was seen to be sufficient. A wave of market-based reforms in the 1980s and 1990s altered many of the service mechanisms of public delivery, but key elements of the Weberian system remained – governments are still strong on hierarchy, formal accountability and controls but weak on engagement – until the later 1990s, when the tide shifted internationally towards a more open and engaged public sector.

From command and control to collaboration

We would like to suggest that rather than the command and control procedures, narrow work restrictions and siloed cultures and operating systems of the traditional bureaucratic model, what needs to (and indeed is beginning to) emerge is a new model characterised by complex networks of multi-organisational, multi-governmental and multi-sectoral collaborations which:

O   recognise the importance of distributed leadership
O   focus first on people and places – not just on programmes and outputs
O   have an eye to sustainability of strategies
O   value local information and networks
O   encourage local priority setting and indeed resource allocation.

For public sector executives, this emerging network governance model will require us to broaden our core responsibilities from managing people and programmes to also providing leadership in coordinating resources that deliver public value.

A renewed interest in communities

Consideration of these changing governance models underpinned the establishment of the Department for Victorian Communities (DVC) in 2002. A key objective of the department is the building of active, confident and resilient communities. These strong communities have a sustainable mix of assets (economic, human, natural and cultural) and strong governance that maximises the equitable use of those assets.

The DVC is part of a global trend. Most regional and central governments are creating departments and offices that focus on community strengthening, community consultation and civic renewal. Some jurisdictions – such as the UK – focus more on the 'renewal of the public realm' and deliberative democracy while others, such as most Australian states, have focused on community strengthening to support mainstream service delivery such as better health education and safety.

The DVC is organised around people and places, not programmes. Core to the brief is to create new forms of collaborative governance. In this context we use the term 'governance' to cover all the decision-making organisations and practices that impact on a community. These include the high-level frameworks and practices of the three levels of government in Australia (local, state and federal) in the way they engage with local communities, to the local management committees of community organisations, school boards, residents groups and business boards.

To do this, strong governance is needed. This is characterised by broad and inclusive networks of decision-makers utilising processes that ensure all the interests within communities wishing to participate have a voice in direction-setting, decision-making and problem-solving. Strong governance is built through connectedness. Network theorists argue healthy communities require a balance of three types of social connection: close personal networks; broader associational ties and community networks; and governance networks. The different network types generate different benefits for individuals and communities and each provides a foundation for building the other.

Communities with strong personal social and civic networks correlate strongly with a range of desirable social and individual characteristics: lower imprisonment rates, higher levels of school completion, and increased participation in economic activity.[2] This research has important policy implications. If network creation can contribute to the reduction of social pathologies or the development of socially desirable attributes then it is interesting that some of the strategies needed to achieve improved outcomes may not be very complex – involving things like encouraging volunteering, investing in social infrastructure, sport, recreation and community arts facilities and even improved streetscaping and attention to local amenities.

What DVC research is beginning to suggest (and notice that we referred to correlations rather than cause and effect) is that investing in communities is really no more (or less) than an approach to prevention or early intervention with the potential (over time) to be a factor in reducing the rate of increase in the demand on some of the most resource-intensive services provided by governments.

The focus on what makes communities stronger enables us to identify not just those community-strengthening strategies we need to invest in, but also allows us to consider the governance arrangements needed to support these investments: how to simultaneously strengthen communities and introduce reforms in the way government works.

Why collaborate?

In Victoria, the answer seems to be that by working together within agencies, across departments or in partnership with others – we can add public value to the resources at hand. This value-adding has a number of dimensions:

- better coordination of investment

O   building the capacity and skills of the people and
     organisations involved
O   extracting economies of scale
O   sharing information and knowledge
O   reducing overlap and duplication
O   engaging others to increase ownership of policy issues
O   building the civic realm.

Through collaborating we have the potential to broaden understanding and commitment to policy solutions, which are critical as
necessary (but not sufficient) conditions in ensuring the outcomes
being pursued are sustainable.

Collaborative approaches need to be encouraged for a reason that
goes to the heart of one of the reasons for the establishment of the
DVC. Individuals and communities don't think in departmental or
programmatic terms. Rather they think about problems to be solved
or issues to be addressed, which as often as not cut across the artificial
boundaries created by organisational boundaries. Our lives are lived
around relationships – work, family and recreation – not around
hundreds of outputs and programmes.

The 'when' of collaboration

So when is collaboration appropriate? We propose six circumstances:

O   where there are complex issues with complex causation
O   when knowledge and resources are required from across
     many sectors
O   when working towards common or related goals
O   where similar planning and delivery systems are in
     operation
O   where there are common clients (individuals, groups,
     communities)
O   when there is a significant allocation of resources over time.

Collaboration strategies should be seen as an extension of our current business models rather than a radically different way of operating. They cover such approaches as multi-ministerial coordination, intra- and interdepartmental cooperation, intergovernmental collaboration, cross-sectoral partnerships and, most challenging of all, the need of agencies to do business through seamless engagement with local communities. To illustrate these various dimensions we will briefly sketch out three areas of collaboration in Victoria, each based around a different approach to collaboration.

Indigenous Affairs policy, a ministerially led approach

Regardless of historical debates, it is evident that the social and economic status of Indigenous Australians today is underpinned by a set of complex factors that act as a significant barrier to addressing the causes of disadvantage in indigenous communities.

In Victoria, Indigenous Affairs typifies the sort of issue that requires strong whole-of-government coordination and effective joining up. The last 30 years of Indigenous Affairs has shown us that single-issue interventions and narrowly focused programmes have had little effect in turning things around. Any positive progress made at the programmatic level has quickly and repeatedly been swamped by the systemic impacts of other factors not addressed by the programme.

As part of its 2002 election policy the government committed itself to a whole-of-government approach to tackling indigenous disadvantage. The development of the model has taken some time, and some of its elements are only now being put in place, personally led by the minister for Aboriginal Affairs.

Key features of the approach involved a two-year consultation with indigenous communities resulting in new representative arrangements. In addition, a Secretaries Group on Indigenous Affairs was established within government to identify and oversee the implementation of cross-departmental indigenous initiatives. Finally, the government is establishing a ministerial taskforce chaired by the deputy premier to provide high-level political support to this endeavour.

In this model we have the nuance of a top-down approach balanced by a concerted effort to engage local communities, focusing effort on new forms of governance and a more seamless approach to service delivery. This illustrates that issues which involve complex systemic and cultural changes require significant and sustained leadership from the top down if they are going to work.

Caroline Springs, working with business and local government

Caroline Springs is a model further removed from the centre of government. It is a growth area community on the western outskirts of Melbourne in the Shire of Melton. Like many growth area suburbs around major metropolitan cities, Caroline Springs faced a number of issues related to the planning, sequencing and development of community infrastructure.[3] In the past these issues tended to get addressed on an ad hoc basis. Now in Caroline Springs, we are doing things differently.[4]

The Caroline Springs partnership model is based on a whole-of-community approach. It involves state and local government working with local community sector agencies and private sector stakeholders, including the local developer Delfin Lend Lease and Bendigo Bank. A project board, based in Caroline Springs, meets regularly. The board deals primarily with the coordination of government and cross-sectoral investments. One of the unique aspects of the Caroline Springs approach has been the joint funding of a place manager by Delfin, DVC and Melton Shire Council.

Though it is still early days, the DVC is pleased with the results achieved to date, including the development of a shared education and community facilities hub (without the partnership there would have been five separate libraries), agreement on open space, planning for sport and recreation facilities, and the commencement of planning for a AU$24-million town precinct.

Key success factors in this model have been the carefully planned and structured partnership between the council, state government and the private sector around a common objective to enhance the overall wellbeing of Caroline Springs. The objective has been to view all potential investment decisions (public and private) through the lens of making the growth area a more active, confident and resilient community.

'A Fairer Victoria' and the Department for Victorian Communities, systemic reforms to support joining up

The models outlined above are largely concerned with the variety of approaches that Victoria is pursuing to tackle specific issues. But our final example highlights the systemic governance reforms that we have been developing to support 'joining up' on the ground. As the models set out below illustrate, the way governance operates is not a peripheral issue – but at the very heart of our collaborative strategy.

One set of reforms designed to promote and strengthen the state's capacity to work in new ways were announced in the Victorian government's social policy framework 'A Fairer Victoria' (AFV) in April 2005.[5] These particular initiatives were:

o *The alignment of departmental regional boundaries into eight administrative regions:* Prior to this each department had a set of unique regional boundaries. While they were similar, small differences meant that departments didn't line up with each other – they also didn't align with local government boundaries. This lack of consistency acted as a brake on establishing stronger working relationships at the regional level.

o *The establishment of regional management forums:* Building on the boundary alignment initiative, AFV introduced a new form of regional governance to Victoria: regional management forums. The forums, which meet quarterly, include state departmental managers and local government CEOs, along with a departmental secretary as regional champion. The role of the forums is to examine critical issues facing the region, encourage cooperation between departments and with councils, and statutory authorities.

O   *A commitment to the greater use of local team-based approaches:* 'A Fairer Victoria' included a commitment to develop community project teams: a new type of administrative arrangement designed to deliver policies in a local setting that require the involvement of more than one department or sector. Community project teams are about creating the administrative flexibility needed to engage communities on complex issues and work with them collaboratively. Teams aim to achieve this within existing public sector management, administration and accountability frameworks.

Together these initiatives are about establishing a platform for simplifying and strengthening governance arrangements for a range of significant public institutions, not least of all state and local government. They create the conditions for stronger communities and focus the scale and scope of joined-up government activity towards local communities.

Culture and skills needed for successful collaboration

These collaborations are requiring us to rethink how we organise and operate as public sector agencies. It also means a rethink of the cultures of our organisations and a re-evaluation of skills and norms which are valued by the leaders and managers of our departments and agencies.

Increasingly, we will need to reward the capacity to work collaboratively both internally and with external partners no less than we reward the one-upmanship which often passes for high-quality policy advice. As the reliance on partnerships and shared intelligence increases across government, as well as between government and other sectors, coordination will need to be more highly valued than control, and alliance-building will become more valued than directing from on high.

This means we will need to promote staff who achieve value through working with others as well as being able to stand out from the crowd because of their conceptual dexterity. We need to reward those who go the extra mile in assisting people to find their way through the incredible opaque maze that is often the public face of government agencies. And we need to go out and listen to the views of people wanting to participate in public debate using consultative processes which suit those people rather than are convenient to us.

These are characteristics which are not evident in the large, complex, organisations that dominate the public sector. They therefore require a conscious, sustained effort on the part of the leaders and managers to change the cultures of our agencies to make them the core behaviours which are valued and rewarded. In our own small way at DVC we are attempting to make this change particularly in the way in which we – both managers and staff – develop the roles of our local presence teams, who work actively with local communities. These teams have four key roles:

O *navigating government:* includes assisting people and organisations to better understand how to access both DVC and other government funding programmes, an orientation by our staff to be door openers rather than gatekeepers

O *brokering:* working with individuals and community organisations to facilitate solutions to problems by bringing together appropriate resources from across government to resolve the issues at hand

O *investment facilitation:* involves working with communities and departments to try to coordinate the flow of investments in ways that make sense from the perspective of the projects or activities being considered rather than being stymied by the artificial silos created by different funding programmes with differing closing dates for application and different criteria often for similar programmes

O *partnerships:* undertaking these activities through the
   creation of collaboration and networks which encourage
   the development of sustainable partnerships in local
   communities.

For DVC staff this approach is a work in progress. And while we can
point to many instances of success we remain acutely aware that old
habits die hard. For us, the central point is that without culture and
skills being addressed the structural and administrative changes
necessary to build successful collaboration simply won't work.

Conclusion

Collaboration requires a rethink of the principles and structures
guiding public administration and the toolkit of public administration. If we were to imagine how one would rethink the way that
government operates to facilitate that objective, then the following six
design principles create a context within which collaboration can
flourish:

O viewing the world through the lens of the service user, be
   they individuals, families or communities (client-focused
   principle)
O developing a simpler or single face of government locally
   (principle of place)
O shifting from government controlling and directing the
   delivery of services to government playing the role of
   facilitator and enabler (principle of enabling)
O devolving of service planning and delivery to the local
   level (principle of subsidiarity)
O developing cross-sectoral approaches to addressing social
   opportunities and problems through partnerships
   between governments, community agencies and the
   corporate sector (principle of partnership)
O harnessing the capacity of local leaders and entrepreneurs
   (principle of local capacity and ownership); not just the

usual suspects, but hearing the voices of people in addition to the peak bodies and organisations which governments usually deal with.

Public administration reform will never be a simple, straightforward process both because of the complexity of the environment in which it happens and because so much of the way public service professionals operate is bound in custom and tradition. But it is also clear that doing business as usual will not deliver the outcomes that the community rightly demands across all levels of government.

This case study has sketched out some of the building blocks of a different way of working. Those of us in leadership roles in the public sector therefore need to lead not only the development of the ideas but also the translation of those ideas into new structures, new instruments, new skills and most importantly new behaviours in our organisations.

It is up to us to render the complex world of government accessible and intelligible, and to establish governance arrangements which enable people to collaborate in setting priorities and implementing arrangements relating to the shape of their communities. There is no 'right' model for collaboration; it is above all else an orientation towards people which requires us to rethink our public sector structures, processes and skills set.

Yehudi Blacher is secretary and David Adams is executive director, strategy and research, both at the Department of Victorian Communities.

Notes

1   M Considine, *Making Public Policy: Institutions, actors strategies* (Melbourne: Policy Press, 2005); and M Bevir and R Rhodes, 'The life, death and resurrection of British governance', *Australian Journal of Public Administration* 65, no 2 (2006).

2   Department for Victorian Communities, *Indicators of Community Strength: A framework and evidence* (Melbourne: DVC, 2006).

3   Victorian Parliament, *Inquiry into Building New Communities*, final report of

the Outer Suburban/Interface Services and Development Committee
(Melbourne: Victorian Parliament, 2006).

4   Department for Victorian Communities, *A Partnership at Caroline Springs in Melton* (Melbourne: DVC, 2006).

5   Victoria State Government, 'A Fairer Victoria: the Victorian government's social policy action plan', 2005 available at
www.dpc.vic.gov.au/CA256D8000265E1A/page/Listing-Publications-
A+Fairer+Victoria+-
+The+Victorian+Government's+social+policy+action+plan!OpenDocument&
1=~&2=~&3=~ (accessed 12 Mar 2007).

Collaboration in action

6. Networked learning communities

Collaboration by design
David Jackson

The twentieth century was the century during which we built large institutions to do things for people. The twenty-first century is the century in which we help people to do things with and for one another.

Stephen Heppell, consultant and former director of
Ultralab at Anglia, Polytechnic University

Some things we know

There is a delightful saying in the organisational learning literature, attributed to Peter Senge, in which he notes that there are some organisations that remain steadfastly unable to learn what everyone in the organisation knows.

Systems are like that, too. Some things we all seem to know, but the systems we work in seem impervious to our collective knowledge. For example, everyone knows that the historical architecture of public service change – delivery, control and accountability – will no longer work. We need to initiate a new way.

The English education system comprises almost 24,000 individual school units, all relatively autonomous, yet accountable to central expectations through a national curriculum, national improvement strategies, key stage testing and inspection regimes. Local market accountabilities, through league tables and parental choice, follow on from these. Together, during the 1990s, these forces combined to render schools more competitive than collaborative. Institutional success became a survival requirement, a stronger imperative than collective success.

Across the English-speaking world, the dominant school improvement models have similar characteristics: schools designed on factory production principles, the profession layered and structured, the system tiered – a hierarchy of school, local authority, state and national agency. Policy is mandated, practices are prescribed, outcome targets specified. The logical route to improvement appears to be to strengthen delivery mechanisms and tighten accountabilities through targets, inspection, financial incentives and consumer choice.

Such 'top-down' approaches are seductive, because they appear to work well in the short term – the system mobilises itself around the targets, teachers teach to the tests – but then improvements stall. More important, although this reform model has been shown to raise general levels of attainment, it has failed to close the gap in educational achievement between the most and the least advantaged.

We know why this is the case. The contexts in which schools work are hugely varied and rapidly changing – centrally coordinated strategies are unlikely to be sensitive to the unique challenges of these diverse circumstances. Such strategies do not stimulate or harness practitioner innovation and ownership. Worse, over time, they can wear down the energy of teachers.

Much we don't yet know

So, there is an increasingly widespread view that a more collaborative, adaptive and long-term problem-solving approach is the way to go. Getting there requires a different model of change: one which emphasises capacity-building, which spreads and uses leadership widely, which enables and encourages rapid knowledge transfer, which fosters and utilises practitioner innovation and creativity, which values system learning and builds for sustainability. The problem is, we just don't yet know how to orchestrate such a pervasive change.

Part of the problem is that policy-makers are heavily influenced by England's history of reform – particularly the more permissive 1960s and 1970s – which would seem to tell us that random, unstructured and unconnected innovation does not serve the system well either. Past experience suggests unfettered innovation is unlikely to achieve the common purpose and connectivity required to bring coherence and alignment to system improvement efforts.

Despite this, there is a history, from different governments, of policies designed to stimulate collaboration, from the Technical and Vocational Education Initiative more than 20 years ago through to Education Action Zones and Excellence in Cities more recently. Most have been heavily prescribed from the centre, mandated, overly incentivised or resource-dependent, and targeted at the most intractable problem areas – inner cities. At best the jury is out as to what we learn from these collaborative policy models, but any sense that there was, by the end of the last century, a cumulative body of knowledge from them would be fanciful.[1]

So, on the ground we don't yet have the practice knowledge to drive change, or the ways of spreading it if we did. Even if we did have clearer understandings of what constituted purposeful and disciplined collaboration, the current architecture of reform mitigates against it. You can't mandate what matters, so what is the role of the central state in promoting and supporting collaborative arrangements?

This was the situation we faced in 2000. Both logic and evidence from practice tell us that purposeful collaboration between schools is better for organisational learning than competition. We wanted to know what effective collaboration looked like, and also how it could be incentivised, mobilised and supported.

Our belief was that networks of schools engaged in orchestrated and disciplined 'networked learning' offered an alternative model for school improvement. We were confident that bringing schools together to develop, share and test new approaches to learning would improve outcomes for young people.

This set of hypotheses lay at the heart of what England's National

College for School Leadership (NCSL) set out to achieve in the Networked Learning Communities (NLC) programme,[2] something I was heavily involved in as the college's head of research and school improvement.

Alternative approaches to incentives and implementation

Launched in 2001, the NLC programme captured a moment. The profession was clearly weary of a climate of competition, outside-in change programmes, normative improvement agendas and externally generated accountability systems. There was a feeling that we needed to create space in the system for local creativity. Having achieved short-term improvements through a centrally driven reform agenda, the next phase would take on different and less predictable shapes.

The programme had a deep philosophical underpinning.[3] All children could be intelligent as long as schools knew how to develop them. The best way for teachers to learn how to do that was for different schools to collaborate – learning and working together across organisational boundaries.

The programme therefore asked schools to form interdependent networks, to work with and for one another for the benefit of the children, the schools and the communities they serve. It was formulated as a 'design intervention' based on international best practice – providing educationalists with the support they needed to build their own networks and develop their own relationships and goals. The aim was to develop engagement and leadership, not to set out new structures.

Documentation was minimal, and intended to support local efforts rather than to meet central requirements. There was funding for the programme, but networks had to match it 'in kind' – showing that they were putting effort and resource into creating lateral learning communities.

We asked people to set out their expected spending on the network, but the only audit was aimed at finding out how the original plans had changed – we wanted to know how the emerging learning was shifting spending decisions over time. There was to be no external review for two years. Instead networks were expected to formulate their learning into 'artefacts' such that knowledge could be shared with other networks. Networks were encouraged to visit one another and practise self- and peer-review.[4] Talking about what didn't work was valued as highly as what did.

Another feature was that networks could not have one leader – co-leadership was the experimental model for the first year, and one which none of the 137 networks moved away from in subsequent years.

Even the process of writing submissions for funding from NCSL was unusual and emphasised learning values. Regional 'submission-writing' seminars were held during which representatives from potential networks helped one another to design proposals through peer critique and the exchange of ideas. The final assessment phase (given that we received 150 proposals – more than ten times what was expected) involved presentation to peer review teams, the thinking being that ideas would be shared and disciplines learned from the assessment process.

The team at NCSL supported the process of developing good networks, capturing learning from the process of building them, and sharing that learning with the wider education system.

So what of value was learned?

Three short sections from the three-year external evaluation of the NLC programme are illuminating. The first states that networks made a difference for young people. They worked to raise achievement:

> There is a connection between the participation in a network and improvement in pupil attainment. . . . The number of people in the school who are active in the network was positively correlated with pupil outcomes . . . and the level of network attachment was related to change in pupil outcomes.[5]

The second explicitly links collaborative activity and joint work with learning and change:

> *Rigorous and challenging joint work may be at the heart of the power of networks. Networks can provide the forum for colleagues to address genuinely new, and often difficult, ideas in a safe environment, away from the risk of censure or even retribution in their daily place of work.*[6]

The third connects learning and leadership – both distributed and formal:

> *Trust relationships and mutual challenge are the things that make the links in networks; tapping explicit (public) knowledge and exposing tacit (private) knowledge provide the process; and leadership, both formal and distributed, can create the forums and provide the necessary support and capacity-building opportunities to move the process forward.*[7]

If this is an overview of the programme, then our work at NCSL helped to pick out a more detailed set of learning points. The first group is a set of 'verities'. The NLC programme drew from the best available knowledge worldwide, and in accumulating that body of evidence, certain themes recurred that have been validated through the work of the programme.

These are, chiefly, that collaboration relies on voluntarism and having a compelling reason to work together – one that can be provided by the strong moral purpose of the teaching profession. Combine this with good internal leadership and external critical friends, and networks can expand access to good ideas and knowledge sharing.

Our ongoing process of learning throughout the programme helped us understand the challenges and rewards of collaboration more deeply. Research and evaluation work highlighted the fact that building networks is far from easy – it requires a large investment of time and energy, and the creation of trusting relationships between the participants, particularly with formal school leaders, who have to engage actively with the process. Trust grows through joint work; it is not a precondition.

But the rewards are worth having – networked learning at its best helped bring to the surface a spirit of reciprocity and generosity. It created a sense of expanded professional identity for the teachers involved, helping them to see themselves as learning on behalf of the profession as a whole.

Beyond this, there are some more tentative propositions that emerged from the NLC work, and which bear the warranty of experience rather than research. Perhaps most importantly, we came across the well-established problem of causality – how can networks prove they are making a difference greater than the sum of their parts, and when they do, how can they take the credit for it?

We knew that voluntarism was vital, but we now believe it can be orchestrated with the help of intermediaries like the NCSL. Successfully orchestrating it relies on good structures built around shared challenges and goals for learning, and in which people are prepared to experiment with new communication channels that break the traditional, hierarchical mould. Logic tells us that ICT should play a vital role in that process, and yet there are no examples of it being integral to the success of networks. As that suggests, networked learning was most likely to work when teachers 'unlearned' some of their old practices and embraced new ways of working.

What did we learn about implementing and facilitating networks?

The team that supported the NLC programme – NCSL's Networked Learning Group – was itself trying to work out what role intermediary bodies could play in catalysing and supporting networks on the ground. Its performance was a potential model for organisations like local authorities in developing collaborative work.

There is no doubt that we did some things well. The programme was both theoretically and practically informed.[8] We succeeded in generating a compelling design, underpinned by values, which motivated engagement. The co-design orientation, and subsequent co-development work, stimulated new relationships between system partners. We didn't have the answers, so these were learning relationships. The 'model of learning' was a seriously important shared discipline. The development team brokered lateral connections and stimulated peer-to-peer learning.

If improved outcomes for children is the critical determinant of success, then the external evaluation shows that this was achieved. If creating a body of knowledge is the yardstick, then it is fair to say that as the programme progressed, we wrestled – successfully on the whole – with the challenges of real-time learning now manifested in our tools and publications. The legacy of products and materials is quite probably of national and international significance.[9]

We never, of course, pretended that we had the answers, or that everything was successful. This was a programme committed to learning through doing, and we were open about our failure with the networks, just as we asked them to be open with one another. With the clarity of hindsight, we could have done a number of things more effectively.

The NLC design was too close to a 'brand'. In proposing NLCs as an ideal prototype to support development, we unwittingly gave the impression that we were proposing this model as the single or best way forward. Again, also with the wisdom of hindsight, our central infrastructure grew too large. Networked systems can be supported with a minimum of central capacity by utilising leadership from the front line – and in so doing grounding decisions and thinking in the experience of practice. Our central infrastructure did not assist us in sustaining the co-development orientation in the eyes of the networks, either.

Two early decisions proved to be only partially correct. First, the networks received nominal funding for the first three of their four-year lifespan. That may have been a mistake. We wanted to stimulate new capacities and ways of working and knew that some funding would help. And so it did, but a proportion of networks saw the removal of funding as a barrier to sustainability. No funding might have been the way to go.

Second, we knew that baselining at the outset would be crucial to evaluating the project's achievements. We wanted each network to take ownership of its own baselining strategy and we developed tools to scaffold that work. Looking back, the work was pretty variable, not least because the networks were at such a formative stage when asked to do it.

The last reflection links into the concluding points below. The network learning group was itself a part of a national agency, NCSL. In common with many innovators, we felt under siege early on, felt that we were challenging historical practices and were in turn being challenged by those who were sceptical or threatened by the programme. We could have integrated our work into the college more effectively – and as a result had less influence there than might have been possible.

That is an honest appraisal. The final section makes some equally honest concluding observations about barriers to taking collaborative practice to scale across whole public service systems.

Conclusion

It is not primarily lack of knowledge that prevents collaborative working – either between schools or across services. The NLC programme alone has created a huge store of evidence[10] and there are other rich sources of knowledge, both in this country and abroad. In a system configured for 'one to many' rather than 'many to many' dissemination, though, there are certainly problems making what knowledge we have widely available sufficiently quickly, at scale, to support emergent practices.

And the issue of scale is also a part of the problem. In her internationally regarded study on scale, Cynthia Coburn identifies four dimensions in which we lack a resolute theory: depth, sustainability, spread and shift in reform ownership.[11] The third of these poses interesting challenges for the support of a collaborative system. About 'spread' she says:

> Rather than thinking of spread solely in terms of expanding
> outward to more and more schools and classrooms, this
> emphasis highlights the potential to spread reform-related
> norms within . . . the district. At the district level, spread involves
> the ways in which reform norms and principles influence district
> policies, procedures, and professional development.[12]

This is a conundrum. We know from our own work that a network-based system requires brokerage and support. There is a crucial facilitation role for local authorities and a critical role in generating facilitative policy at a national level. To make the shift, both local and national agencies will have to internalise the challenging 'norms and principles' of a more networked and collaborative system. But local and national government often appear irretrievably hierarchical and bureaucratic.

Returning for a moment to the epigraph at the start of this piece, Stephen Heppell referred to the organisations set up in the twentieth century to do things for people. As we seek to liberate collaborative arrangements, to help people to do things with and for one another, what could well stand in the way are those same organisations, hierarchically structured, culturally siloed, relatively impermeable to learning, set up to provide answers and to believe that they know best.

If this applies to local authorities, it is equally applicable to national agencies, to government and to the structures of the civil service. The critical orientation for change is a learning orientation. This means engagement with frontline collaborative practices, not to provide answers, not to hold to account, or to bureaucratise, but to learn how better to accommodate risk, and to provide enablement and support. It is the role of system broker and shaper, and it is a very different orientation.

David Jackson is the former director of the Networked Learning Group, National Collection for School Leadership.

Notes

1   Demos/National College for School Leadership, *Learning the Lessons: How past policy initiatives can help practitioners in the Networked Learning Communities programme* (Nottingham: NCSL, 2002), available at http://networkedlearning.ncsl.org.uk/knowledge-base/research-papers/learning-the-policy-lessons.pdf (accessed 14 Mar 2007).

2   D Jackson, 'Networked Learning Communities: the role of knowledge-based networks in school and system improvement', paper presented at the CERI/OECD forum, 'Knowledge management in education and learning', March 2002, see www.ncsl.org.uk/nlc (accessed 10 Mar 2007); and D Jackson, 'Learning themes from the Networked Learning Communities programme', paper presented at the International Congress for School Effectiveness and Improvement Conference, Barcelona, 2–5 Jan 2005, see www.ncsl.org.uk/nlc (accessed 10 Mar 2007).

3   NCSL, *Like No Other Initiative* (Nottingham: NCSL, 2003), available at www.ncsl.org.uk/nlc (accessed 10 Mar 2007).

4   See NCSL, *Getting Started with Network Study Visits*, available at www.ncsl.org.uk/nlc (accessed 10 Mar 2007).

5   L Earl et al, *How Networked Learning Communities Work*, final report of the three-year external evaluation of the Networked Learning Communities programme (Nottingham: NCSL, 2006), available at www.ncsl.org.uk/nlc (accessed 10 Mar 2007).

6   Ibid.

7   Ibid.

8   R McCormick, *Theoretical Perspectives of Relevance to Networked Learning Communities* (Nottingham: NCSL, 2002), available at www.ncsl.org.uk/nlc (accessed 10 Mar 2007).

9   See www.ncsl.org.uk/nlc (accessed 10 Mar 2007).

10   Ibid.

11   C Coburn, 'Rethinking scale: moving beyond numbers to deep and lasting change', *Educational Researcher* 32, no 6 (Aug/Sep 2003).

12   Ibid.

7. Learning together

The collaborative college
Sarah Gillinson, Celia Hannon and Niamh Gallagher

Networks make the college – those relationships are key, they're not optional.

Peter Mayhew-Smith, head of general education,
Lewisham College

Lewisham College specialises in providing second chances for local people. And, as this case study shows, they are very good at it. The college's 2006 Ofsted report was littered with 'outstanding' and 'excellent' and all but one of its grades was at the highest possible level. Staff have beacon status in a variety of areas and the college has been designated a 'centre of vocational excellence'.

But crucially, this is not a story of high-quality provision and innovation in an area where it is 'easy' to make it happen. The London Borough of Lewisham is the 15th most deprived in the UK and less than 50 per cent of young people gain five GCSEs at A* to C grades. As the principal puts it, 'we're not interested in making silk purses out of silk purses'. What they are interested in is 'opening up education to as many people as possible . . . and encouraging them to continue and to succeed'.

That is why they collaborate. Because without partnerships, the college would never be able to reach young people in the local community, including the large numbers who were either excluded from school, or who stayed but were seriously demotivated by the experience. And without strong links to the 'real world' of business, the college would find it much harder to help those young people into good jobs. As Peter Mayhew-Smith, head of general education, says, 'the only way to get these learners is by working closely with Connexions, social services and housing associations'.

Of course, the college could function perfectly well without its partnerships, but it would be a very different place. The danger, as Mayhew-Smith points out, is that the college would end up simply teaching people who were already interested in getting an education, rather than reaching new students who might not previously have considered investing in their own skills.

The college recognises the value of an informal conversation, a one-off venture, joint bids for funding and long-term strategic agreements. They involve a huge variety of players in the community including local schools, trade unions, local employers, community groups, Connexions, the fire service, other colleges nationally, and Job Centre Plus among others.

Pippa Lusby, the college's programme area leader for sport and recreation, is clear that this mutual benefit might be a simple exchange of resources. She needs 'live bodies' – young people with whom her trainee sports coaches can gain practical experience. Local primary schools need trained and enthusiastic physical education support. So several local schools come to the college's sports hall once a week for coaching, which is often one to one – there are as many trainee coaches as pupils. Children love it and their teachers are thrilled – they are freed up to do the marking they might otherwise take home.

Local employers get a similarly good deal in working with the college – the City Bound programme is built on partnerships with high-profile corporations including Deloitte, Morgan Stanley and HSBC. College programme leaders customise training programmes by talking to businesses about the skills they need – from punctuality to literacy levels. In return, participating businesses offer internships to the programme's students, with the understanding that if they perform well, they have a high chance of being employed. The programme has an eventual employment rate of 70 per cent.

Partnering locally

The college's strategic partnerships with other local services are still developing, but they could eventually make a major impact on the community. Key players from the fire service, police, primary care trust and others meet regularly with the aim of understanding where their offers overlap, either duplicating or complementing one another. Each member is currently undertaking a year-long audit of their impact in the most deprived areas of the community.

As Geoff Sorrell, the deputy principal, put it, 'we need to understand the implications of all our people on the ground'. They know that the impact they make is interdependent – that how health care is done affects someone's readiness to learn, or that going to college 'stops kids from setting fire to cars' as Dame Ruth Silver, the principal, pointed out.

This work is still very much in its early stages – but the group believes that in the long term, their partnership will help maximise the impact of their collective spending on a shared goal – supporting community members to improve the quality of their lives. In the meantime, the arrangement has meant that informal, smaller-scale, 'one-off' exchanges can also be made, such as securing more work placements at the council for Lewisham students.

So from micro to macro, whoever or whatever is involved, the reason for collaboration is simple: to contribute to achieving the college's mission and 'push prosperity for all our communities by widening participation to learning opportunities that enrich personal, cultural and social development and which will enable participation in economic life'.

Collaboration with other further education colleges

Lewisham College is a founding member of the 'League for Learning' – a national partnership with other high-performing colleges. This selective approach is characteristic of how Lewisham approaches collaboration; the College identified a weakness in its own knowledge about work-based learning, and set about identifying those with particular strength in this area, drawing on their expertise. It reciprocated with its own areas of excellence. This knowledge-sharing exercise has enabled Lewisham to restructure its work-based learning programme and make radical changes – outcomes for learners improved by 43 per cent over the 2005/06 academic year. As Geoff Sorell noted, the beginning of this process can be as simple as 'sitting around the table and asking each other: what works for you and why?'

Shared goals and exchanging resources lie at the heart of most successful collaborations, but they are seldom enough on their own. Interpersonal relationships, strong shared values and trust are critical too, something the college understands. At the heart of its work is a non-negotiable focus on the learner and the community the college serves, and most of its partnerships are built on that foundation.

College staff emphasise the significance of clarity of purpose – in any relationship, both parties need to understand their objectives and how they plan to achieve them. Delivering quality results in line with these agreements is essential for maintaining Lewisham's excellent reputation. Mark Cooke, the head of business development, argues that setting the parameters early on improves the relationship in the long run: 'It's important to do what you say you'll do.' In turn, this means the college has no shortage of potential partners.

Listening and understanding are crucial to setting realistic and effective targets from the beginning. Leaders at every level of the organisation were very clear about the danger of making assumptions about other people's needs. When the college began a training programme with Belmarsh prison employees, Dawn, the course leader, shadowed potential learners to understand the pattern of their day, working environment and accepted 'lingo' as well as their learning requirements. As she said: 'You have to live it to understand it.' As a result, they offer a round-the-clock, on-site service that has won a beacon award.

The college also works hard to sustain its innovative range of partnerships over the long term. Collaborative relationships often do not happen organically – they demand considerable perseverance. Communication is vital to this – almost all Lewisham College's staff pinpointed clear communication channels with their partners as essential to identifying and tackling problems before they arise. The Business Development Department has appointed a dedicated 'relationship manager' responsible for the health of its partnerships.

Finally, every member of staff we spoke to at Lewisham had an approach to forming external partnerships which was firmly rooted in an ambitious sense of curiosity – whether that entailed knocking on several doors until they found what they needed or simply being open to all possibilities. Rossina remarked that she had 'never said no, that's just the style of the college – it's a very creative atmosphere'.

Collaborating internally

But the college's strong external relationships are not just a question of building and maintaining partnerships – its connections to the outside world are also rooted in a strong culture of collaboration within the college. 'Boundaries within the college are low' as the head of general education told us – colleagues can approach each other for help and support in realising ambitious external projects.

Perhaps most importantly, there is leadership from the top. The principal is clearly committed to improving the surrounding community, and she is backed up by governors who are ready to support the frontline risk-taking essential for innovation. Everyone knows it and it colours the entire college. As several interviewees put it: 'You know what you're signing up to.' The internal and external clarity of purpose attracts and motivates the people who share its values; the organisation is 'fractal' says the principal – we all share a little bit of each other.

As that suggests, the principal's strong vision does not act as a centralising force, building the whole college around a charismatic individual. Quite the opposite. A widely shared set of core values liberates the college to have what the principal calls 'lateral leadership'. Departments and individuals can be free to respond imaginatively to particular challenges in their areas where a shared purpose generates the coherence that holds all these strands together.

This is possible because there is a sense that 'the college is bigger than you'. There is a shared feeling that all its members are on a quest to pursue prosperity for the local community, and this overrides any sense of territorialism between departments.

Secure in its values and direction, the college seems to have been able to get into the habit of managing change. Being flexible and adaptable has become a way of life. The leadership team changes the structure of the college every year to make it more fit for 'purpose, context and change' as the principal put it. So new circumstances or new community groups to integrate into the life of the college do not automatically undermine its modus operandus – they are simply a new challenge.

Finally, the value of 'difference', and complementary skills and interests, is embedded in the college's make up. The principal purposefully recruits on the basis of difference and diversity, as much as on the shared values discussed earlier. Recognising the value of working with different organisations and individuals externally is simply an extension of internal practices.

The importance of context

The external climate is also influential. Political, social, economic and historical factors are all important in creating an environment in which successful and mutually beneficial collaboration can flourish.

The political environment has undoubtedly played a role as a trigger, if not the foundation of some external partnership work. Government policy requires certain bids to be made in collaboration with other organisations in the borough. While this can create artificial alliances, staff at Lewisham College also point out the value behind creating these channels, which allow the college to get out into the community. Staff spoke of several examples of 'compulsory' collaboration about which they had initially been extremely sceptical but which have blossomed into 'real' relationships over time, even without government money to sustain them.

Social factors form some of the most important roots of successful collaboration. There is community-wide recognition of and a sense of moral responsibility about the mutual interdependence of the public services at the heart of the community. From working across the Local Strategic Partnership in a formal structure, to more informal partnerships around sport, business and industry, the motivating factor is the knowledge that no single organisation alone can improve quality of life across the borough.

This is compounded by the 'localness' of the community. Many staff and students live, work, learn and get ill in local schools, hospitals and housing. This constant interaction with the same group of people enables the 'tentacles' of the college to reach out across the community, into neighbourhoods, schools, prisons and businesses and highlights the ongoing interdependence of people and services. Partnerships are conceived, emerge and develop at the school gate, on the shop floor or over the phone with a local doctor. The professional and the personal continuously overlap, making Lewisham ripe and obvious turf for collaboration.

The economic environment also has a part to play. Lewisham is not a rich borough – it has high levels of deprivation, ethnic minorities and lone parents, and low levels of literacy and numeracy. These economic and social factors mean that partnerships generally attract government funding. So there are economic as well as moral arguments for collaboration.

Finally, Lewisham College has a history of partnership work. Now almost 100 years old, the college was run by the local authority until 1992. There is a 'residue' of the strong relationships between local government and 'delivery' organisations as a result.

All of these factors create an interdependent web on which successful, ongoing collaboration is founded in Lewisham. Some of these are non-negotiable, like that spirit of curiosity that makes partnership working a natural reaction. Some simply contribute by 'suggesting a direction', as the head of general education put it, like government policy – factors like these would see collaboration founder if they alone were depended on to make it work.

So collaboration at Lewisham is not an optional extra. Staff at the college look outside their departments and beyond the organisation as a matter of course, to access, understand and serve their local community. As the principal says, they do not just see their work affecting 'learners'. They help people to build skills, confidence, relationships and aspiration – they work to make the whole community a safer, happier and more prosperous place. In short, they work with the community, to empower the community. They could not do it alone.

Sarah Gillinson, Celia Hannon and Niamh Gallagher are Demos researchers.

8. Your experience matters

Designing healthcare with citizens
Lynne Maher

You have to get there early to claim a seat otherwise you're standing. . . . By the time the consultants arrive at the clinic it is already busy as the clinic shares its waiting area. The patients and carers are standing all over the place, waiting to be seen.

This was before collaboration. Now, at Luton and Dunstable Hospital Head and Neck Cancer Services things are very different. Patients, carers, hospital staff, researchers, anthropologists and designers are working together to create a truly user-led service. The waiting area is designed according to patients' needs, appointment flows are arranged so as to avoid crowding, and together staff and patients are trialling how the clinic space is used – instead of consultants having rooms, which patients move in and out of, patients now have rooms and staff move to see them. All of this is part of an innovative work in progress aiming to build genuinely user-led services based on collaboration.

Many of the case studies in this collection describe collaboration between different organisations. This essay focuses on collaboration within the context of a public sector organisation, an acute hospital trust, operating within the National Health Service (NHS).

The NHS is a large and complex organisation which is seen with a sense of importance by the nation. It is currently in the middle of a ten-year reform programme, the ambitions of which are set out in

The NHS Plan.[1] Improvement collaboratives – where members of a multidisciplinary health team work together with a commitment to improving services – have emerged as a popular tactic for change. The impact of these collaboratives has already been demonstrated in a number of ways in England, including significantly reducing waiting times and streamlining services.[2]

Within health service collaboratives, there is a core group of team members with responsibility for a particular service. For example a collaborative focused on improving an outpatient service is likely to involve a range of staff including nurses, clinic clerks, diagnostic services staff, doctors, secretaries and managers. The majority of these initiatives have taken great care to collect and integrate user's views into the redesign of services; however, there are fewer examples where users are involved in a fully integrated way; that is where Luton and Dunstable is different.

The government understands the need to collaborate with patients. The recent *Creating a Patient-led NHS*[3] document calls for a fundamental change in our relationships with patients in order to 'move from a service that does things to and for its patients to one which is patient-led where the service works with patients to support them with their health needs'.

Yet the language used in the document remains focused on traditional methods of engagement (see figure 1), where the patient experience is often as a passive recipient. Creating a patient-led NHS cannot be done by simply 'providing choice, and using the skills of listening, understanding and responding'; these are more traditional methods of patient engagement, and do not engage the patient in a collaborative way – they can be described as the rhetoric. Now, we need to make way for the reality of active collaboration with users of healthcare services leading the way.

The ongoing improvement of health services is a high priority for politicians, healthcare staff and citizens alike. Existing perspectives, methods and approaches (and the underlying theories that drive them) cannot be relied on to deliver the required change in the time and on the scale required.[4] It is time to move the focus so that

Figure 1 The continuum of citizens' influence

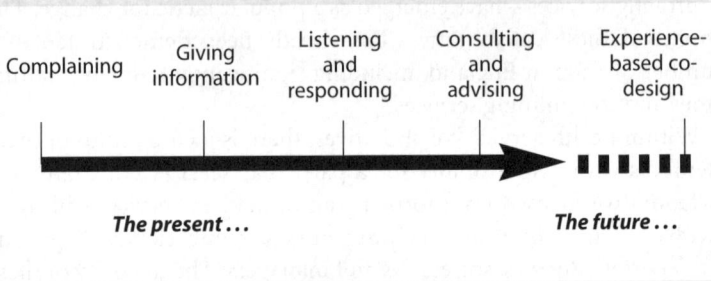

Source: SP Bate and G Robert, 'Experience-based design: from redesigning the system around the patient to co-designing services with the patient', *Quality and Safety in Health Care* 15, no 5 (2006).

healthcare services are truly focused on the needs of patients and carers. This case study, which outlines the experience of the head and neck cancer service at the Luton and Dunstable Hospital NHS Trust, illustrates how using design principles and collaborative approaches can revolutionise the experience of patients and carers.

At Luton and Dunstable we have taken an innovative approach to the ongoing redesign of our service, by putting patients and staff right at the centre of the process. Using the concept of 'experience-based design' we draw on the actual experiences of our users. Patients and carers are invited to tell stories about their experience of our service; these stories provide insights which enable the designers to think about designing experiences rather than designing services.[5] By 'designers' we mean all of those involved in the collaborative: patients, staff, researchers, improvement leaders and, of course, design professionals.

For us, defining people's experience of our service means asking a series of questions: How well do they understand the service? How do they feel about it while they are using it? How well does it serve its purpose? And how well does it fit into the context in which they are using it? By identifying the main areas or 'touchpoints' where people come into contact with the service, where their experience is shaped, we can identify where the desired emotional and sensory connection needs to be established. Then, by working with people in the front line – doctors, nurses and hospital administrative staff – we can begin to design experiences rather than just systems or processes.[6]

The approach taken by the head and neck cancer service at Luton and Dunstable ensures that the patient and carer are not limited to the traditional role of passive recipient. Instead, patients and carers are active participants in the co-design of their services, as illustrated at the far right-hand side of figure 1. Co-design means that all of those involved in the collaborative play an active role. For example, patients and carers have changed project documentation so that it better reflects their needs, and clinic staff and patients have worked together to redesign the flow of outpatients in the consulting room.

Various methodologies were used to encourage patient involvement in the process, including patient interviews, log books and filmmaking. This enabled patients to show the experience of the service through their own lens, and bring their story to life for others.

Patients found this an incredibly powerful way to share their stories and be heard. When the films were shown during work sessions it immediately created a shared understanding and a new empathy for the deeper needs of patients. The effect was to connect and energise the group towards a common purpose – to improve the patient, carer and staff experience. Now, film has become part of the user journey itself, an example of how handing over control to users to inspire collaboration can become an aspect of the service in its own right.

Through our collaborative project at Luton and Dunstable, we aimed to answer three questions:

1   How can we design healthcare services that really meet the needs of patients?
2   How can we move away from the current ideal of a 'satisfied customer'?

Figure 2 Project structure and work flow

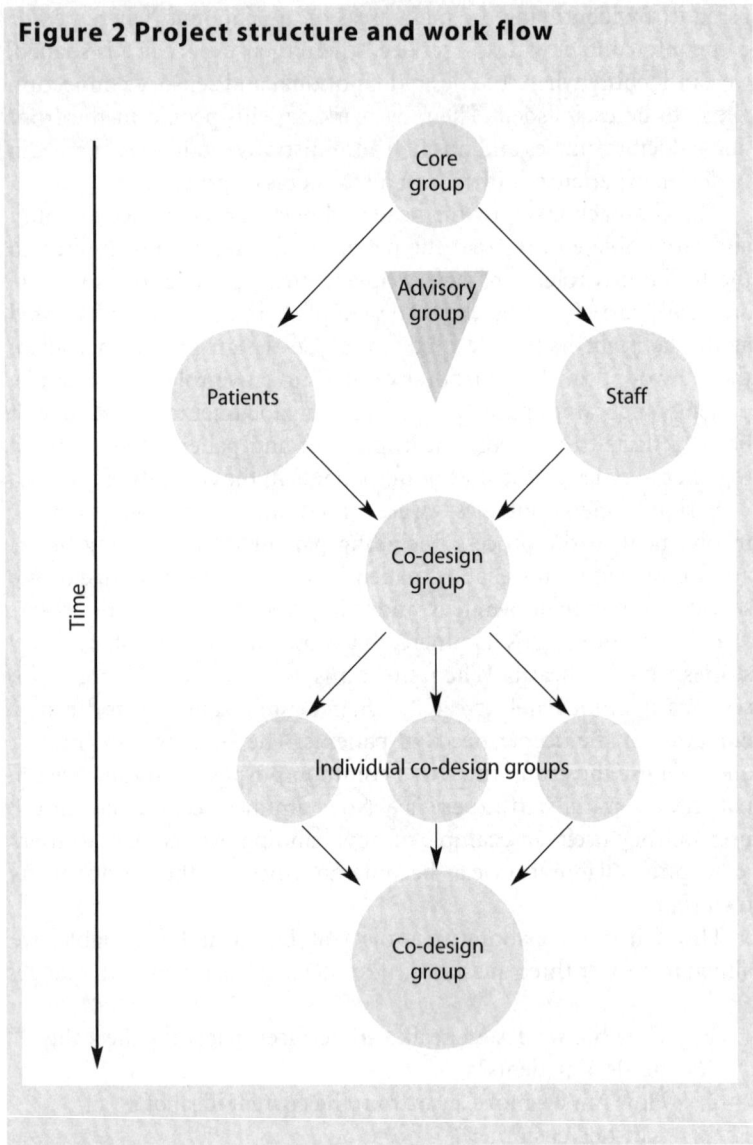

3   How can we create and provide an exceptional experience?

While a central element of the work was to ensure that patients and carers were core and active team members, we also recognised the need to harness the collective wisdom of all participants in order to maximise the potential for improvement. We chose to use the notion of co-design as a key principle, with a strong emphasis for change based on the experience of those who used the service.

The selection of people who act as co-designers makes for an unusual mix of expertise when considered within the healthcare environment. However, the process was enriched by taking into consideration the different skills, views and life experiences of the patients, carers and others involved. Often in the health service we forget that patients have lives outside of their illness and that their wealth of expertise is available to us. Once recognised, these skills and experiences provided the head and neck cancer service with a vast pool of collective wisdom, both from within and outside of healthcare.

How did it work?

To make the collaborative at Luton and Dunstable work it was critical to create a 'mechanism' through which each of the participants were able to put forward their views and contribute fully in the resulting change process. We designed a structure that served two purposes: it formally enabled contribution, through specific groups, and it also formed our work flow over the course of the project (see figure 2).

The Core group represents the broad range of participants and has a central role in managing and facilitating the project. It is here that reflection on learning is shared, next steps are planned and changes are made. At least two members of the Core group are available for every interaction within the project.

The Advisory group provides the governance structure for the project and provides advice to ensure the project consistently meets its aims.

The Patients group also includes carers. Both have identified, through stories of their experiences of receiving care, aspects of the service that they would like to see kept or changed. Some of those involved in the patients group are also members of the Advisory group.

The Staff group is made up of all grades of staff who are involved in the process of care that patients experience. They have a remit to identify aspects, through their experiences of providing or delivering care, that they feel need to be improved or retained.

The Co-design group involves the Core group, Patients group and Staff group. Through this, patients, carers, staff, designers, anthropologists and improvement experts meet together to listen to each others' experiences and identify areas to work on. Each action to be taken was clearly defined and had a nominated person to lead the work within an individual co-design group.

Individual Co-design groups are working on each of the individual actions. Some of these groups consist of only two or three people, while some involve eight to ten people. The leadership responsibility is shared by participants of the collaborative.

The final Co-design group will come together to celebrate the achievements and learning and to plan for the next steps after the formal project has ended.

The initial Co-design group identified 38 different actions to be taken, all based on user experience. Great care is taken to explicitly link the experience to the action by using actual narrative as expressed by patients or carers; this helps to retain the 'story' that has influenced the change. Many of the changes requested by patients required tiny measures, for example staff moved the weighing scales out of sight of the waiting room; they hadn't noticed how embarrassing patients found it to be weighed in front of everyone. The impact of such a small gesture is potentially huge when people's experiences of the service are mapped. Other actions, such as changing the way the clinic space is used, have required more thought or organisation, yet many of these have been achieved quickly and inexpensively while still resulting in a significant difference to the patient experience.

Some actions are much more complex, and require more time, coordination, consideration of and integration with existing structures and systems within the organisation. These actions remain a 'work in progress', and steps so far include changing the location of equipment and resources so that they are more accessible to staff, and ensuring that patient lockers are free for patients to use when necessary.

What it means

Some people believe that by involving patients and carers in this way the health service will be exposed to expensive demands that it will be unable to meet. In our experience this has not been the reality. Rather, a large number of small and inexpensive changes have significantly improved the service provided to our users. This is supported by the view of Derek Wanless who states that 'putting patients in control and helping them to be fully engaged in their healthcare is likely to be more cost effective and offer better value for money than if people are simply passive recipients of services'.[7] At Luton and Dunstable we have found this to be true.

As one member of our team points out: 'Patients and staff are not asking for gold taps, in fact most of their suggestions are quite achievable with little budget. I would say that one of the most important things is providing space for relationships to build and supporting that with communication.'

At Luton and Dunstable we have moved from the rhetoric of involving patients in our efforts to improve health services, which is often limited to attendance at a focus group or filling out a questionnaire, to the reality of co-designing, not only with healthcare service users but also with staff, researchers, designers and others with valuable expertise. It is through this method of co-design that we can really achieve a health service that meets the needs of those who need it.

Lynne Maher is head of innovation practice, NHS Institute for Innovation and Improvement.

Notes

1   Department of Health, *The NHS Plan: A plan for investment, a plan for reform* (London: DoH, 2000), available at www.dh.gov.uk/PublicationsAndStatistics/Publications/PublicationsPolicyAndGuidance/PublicationsPolicyAndGuidanceArticle/fs/en?CONTENT_ID=4002960&chk=07GL5R (accessed 14 Mar 2007).

2   D Kerr et al, 'Redesigning cancer care', *BMJ* 324 (2002).

3   Department of Health, *Creating a Patient-led NHS: Delivering the NHS improvement plan* (London: DoH, 2005), available at www.dh.gov.uk/PublicationsAndStatistics/Publications/PublicationsPolicyAndGuidance/PublicationsPolicyAndGuidanceArticle/fs/en?CONTENT_ID=4106506&chk=ftV6vA (accessed 14 Mar 2007).

4   SP Bate, G Robert and H McCloud, *A Report on the 'Breakthrough' Collaborative Approach to Quality and Service Improvement within Four Regions of the NHS* (Birmingham: Health Service Management Centre at Birmingham University, 2002).

5   BJ Pine and JH Gilmore, *The Experience Economy* (Boston, MA: Harvard Business School Press, 1999); and BH Schmitt, *Customer Experience Management: A revolutionary approach to connecting with your customers* (San Francisco, CA: Wiley, 2003).

6   SP Bate and G Robert, 'Experience-based design: from redesigning the system around the patient to co-designing services with the patient', *Quality and Safety in Health Care* 15, no 5 (2006).

7   D Wanless, *Securing Our Future Health: Taking a long-term view* (London: HM Treasury, 2002), available at www.hm-treasury.gov.uk/consultations_and_legislation/wanless/consult_wanless_final.cfm (accessed 14 Mar 2007).

9. Katrina's code

How online collaboration tools came to the rescue in New Orleans
Paul Miller and Niamh Gallagher

On 29 August 2005, Hurricane Katrina decimated the American city of New Orleans. The storm ripped through the region, causing the worst natural disaster in living memory. It caused over a thousand deaths, displaced millions of people and racked up billions of dollars worth of damage. More than a year on, much of the city has yet to fully recover.

The disaster proved to be a ferocious test for government and, in particular, for the Federal Emergency Management Agency (FEMA). Its director at the time, Michael Brown, came in for intense criticism and was eventually forced to leave his role.

His problem, like many decision-makers in the aftermath of a disaster, was getting access to accurate and timely information. Even the best-laid plans of the most experienced emergency specialists can be swept aside by confusion. FEMA only found out that thousands of citizens were trapped in the New Orleans Superdome when officials saw it on the TV news.

Eight months later, a report by the Department of Homeland Security's inspector general was damning – during the hours and days that followed the storm, Brown's team just didn't know what was going on.

But outside the structures and agencies of government, the lack of reliable information led to the creation of some unusual solutions that might point to new forms of collaboration for the future. For the first time, online tools were used in a concerted way by concerned citizens to help the victims of a major disaster.

Technology meant that citizens could do more than just give money (which wasn't the major problem anyway) – they could use their skills and time to produce real benefits for the victims of the disaster through online collaborative tools.

As the author Steven Johnson has written about the episode: 'What's striking about this movement is how much it differs from the traditional civilian response to natural disasters. Instead of sending clothes or food or dollars, next-generation volunteers supply data.'[1]

The bottom-up response to the crisis of information surrounding Katrina began to work almost immediately. Within just a few days online volunteers had processed 50,000 entries about missing or displaced people. Their efforts also provided information about temporary housing, allowing people around the country to offer spare accommodation to people who had lost their homes. Within just a few days, the system had found shelter for 5000 people.

An instant message

The weekend after the hurricane struck, tech-savvy activists began to email each other to work out what they could do to help. They realised that although information was being posted about missing people on sites like craigslist and Yahoo!, there was no common resource that people could go to. So they organised a volunteer effort to collate the data, both automatically and manually, and put it into a standard format so people could search accurately.

David Geilhufe of the Social Source Foundation (a nonprofit organisation that exists to create open source software for the nonprofit sector) started gathering the data by 'screen scraping' – an automated process that involves grabbing the relevant information for each person – name, location, age and description – from different sites across the internet. The data was deposited in a single database with a standardised data format called PeopleFinder.

At the same time, Jon Lebkowsky and Ethan Zuckerman decided to team up to coordinate a volunteer effort to collate all the information that couldn't be screen-scraped. Lebkowsky recruited people to scan through all the online posts about the disaster, while Zuckerman dealt out chunks of data to be analysed.

With the standard in place and a small army of volunteers making sure as much data as possible was available, people looking for relatives or friends could visit www.katrinalist.net, enter a name, a postcode, or an address and get a list of names matching the query and their whereabouts within seconds.

As Steven Johnson wrote in *Discover* magazine: 'PeopleFinder was the kind of data-management effort that could have taken a year to execute at great expense if a corporation or a government agency had been in charge of it. The PeopleFinder group managed to pull it off in four days for zero dollars.'[2]

In fact, the PeopleFinder group didn't manage it on their own. It had to collaborate with existing organisations such as Salesforce.com, which provides customer relationship management software, to provide the katrinalist service.

However, project leaders were hesitant to form a relationship with the Red Cross, whose database was built with assistance from Microsoft.

Jon Lebkowsky writes in the Smart Mobs blog: 'Marty Kearns of Network Centric Advocacy encouraged the PeopleFinder project to throw its data to Red Cross and to push for the Red Cross site to be the single authoritative search for evacuees and other Katrina victims, and family and friends searching for them. Marty's suggestion implied a difficult question: should the PeopleFinder project end?'[3]

In the end, PeopleFinder decided against it, at least in part because they thought their service was better designed and more reliable than anything the professionals had managed to create.

Meanwhile, web designers in Utah launched a site called www.katrinahousing.org to connect evacuees with people all across the country who had a spare bedroom or a guest cottage or even a foldout couch. Two weeks later, 5000 people had found temporary homes through the site.

Another group set up improvised wireless networks in damaged areas, distributing computers and 'voice over IP' phones to storm victims and first responders, and establishing low-power FM radio stations in places like the Astrodome. According to the Champaign-Urbana Community Wireless Network home page, the groups involved in the project shipped well over a tonne of equipment to the region within days.

None of the tools that were used were expensive or particularly high-tech. It was much more a case of providing an easy way for people to help without putting themselves in danger or getting in the way of the authorities.

Web wisdom

The volunteer projects that developed in the aftermath of Katrina can teach us a lot about how online collaborative tools might be best used in the future and how the state should relate to citizens using collaborative tools in less troubled times. There are four aspects of the episode that we need to understand: the motivation of the volunteers, the importance of scale, the kinds of leadership required, and the new models of knowledge sharing they used.

Motivation

What drove people to provide their time and skills for free? Obviously people wanted to help because they felt empathy for the people that were in need. This was a disaster that people could identify with, and the online projects provided an outlet for their desire to help.

It was also important that the volunteer task was time limited. Help was needed fast, but only for a finite period of a few days or weeks. The organisers weren't asking people to give up their day jobs forever, they were asking them to provide a few hours here and there.

There was also an element of pride and confidence among the volunteers that they could do a better job than the professionals. This competitive drive among talented amateurs is a common sentiment and one that is often overlooked. We believe so heavily in the primacy of professionals that we underplay the role of people who can be just as disciplined, motivated and knowledgeable, and who often take pride in the fact that they can and do provide their skills for free.

Scale

One of the major differences in the technological landscape during the response to Katrina – compared with previous disasters – was the availability of cheap, reliable, easy-to-use online tools. These allowed many more people to collaborate than would be possible using phones, fax or even email. Blogs and wikis allow many-to-many communication and collaboration allowing thousands, if not millions, of people to share information and take action.

James Surowiecki's much-cited book *The Wisdom of Crowds* has virtually become a mode of organisation for the technology activists.[4] When it comes to information, their slogan is that 'many eyes make bugs shallow' – cleverly organised projects involving millions of volunteers can do a better job than conventionally organised hierarchies. Government responses may require only limited numbers of people, working in precise chains of command, but bottom-up responses like PeopleFinder thrive on many people working together with very fuzzy systems of accountability.

Leadership

Jimmy Wales, the founder of Wikipedia, is sometimes referred to as a benign dictator – a leadership approach that has many similarities to the role of the lead organisers in the Katrina response.[5]

These lead organisers have an innate knowledge of how to leverage what Yale law professor and author of *The Wealth of Networks*, Yochai Benkler, calls social production.[6] This is activity not determined by price signals (through pay or incentives) or by compulsion (through organisational contracts or the law). Instead, social producers know how to build, maintain and channel people's latent enthusiasm and motivation that we highlighted above.

Lead organisers rely on one of the major advantages of commons-based peer production – that it is based on decentralised information gathering and exchange. As a volunteer, you can sign up to help in the ways you feel comfortable doing, rather than being told what to do. As Benkler writes, this model of production 'places the point of decision about assigning any given person to any given set of resources with the individual'.[7]

Knowledge sharing

Yochai Benkler also argues that the presence of an open, common set of resources and knowledge is required for effective social production. In the case of the Katrina response, there was no shortage of online information available to volunteers about how to be part of the whole enterprise. It was easy, using message boards, wikis and blogs to explain how to get involved and how to get round specific problems or challenges.

One of the key success factors in social production is setting standards by which collaborators will abide. These standards don't often emerge instantaneously and often involve an understanding of usability and the social norms of particular situations. It's only now, for example, several years into the Wikipedia project, that real standards for articles are beginning to evolve. But in the case of PeopleFinder, a standard was needed (and imposed) straight away.

A growing power

There is little doubt that the tech response to Katrina simply wouldn't have been possible five years ago. Technology, and a large number of users' mastery of the technology, has advanced so quickly that new opportunities for online tools are being found all the time. Of course, this trend is only likely to grow as technology and high-speed internet connections become more ubiquitous.

The phrase – loved by some, loathed by others – that has come to describe many of the online social tools that have become popular in recent years is 'Web 2.0'.

Tim Berners Lee, the creator of the world wide web argues that Web 2.0 is just a realisation of the features built into the web from day one.[8] Whether that's true or not, there is a new energy around tools like blogs, wikis and other online services that come with participation and collaboration as standard.

Many of the tools described as Web 2.0 are overtly designed to help people cooperate. Blogs make publishing simple, allowing people to get a message or a story into the public domain quickly, and allow comments and links to other websites to add context and debate to the discussion. Wikis allow users to co-author webpages and hence collaborate on the creation of information sources.

So perhaps it's no surprise that Jeff Jarvis (and others since) have described PeopleFinder and other similar projects as 'Recovery 2.0'.[9] There's even an effort to learn from past attempts and set up a Recovery 2.0 initiative wiki. The wiki is a collection point for information about open source disaster recovery.

The project's goal is to be ready for the next disaster so people can 'use the internet to better: share information; report and act on calls for help; coordinate relief; connect the missing; provide connections for such necessities as housing and jobs; match charitable assets to needs; and get people connected to these projects – and the world – sooner.'[10]

While specific statistics are difficult to come by, most commentators agree that there has been a growth in online volunteering in recent years. And the signs are that the generation of young people currently in school are even more at ease with new digital technologies than the generation from which the lead organisers of the Katrina response came from. For them it may become increasingly natural to offer their time as online volunteers rather than just giving money or volunteering in the real world.

There are also signs that non-governmental organisations and development agencies are increasingly experimenting with online tools, particularly through their own websites. At the moment, though, their primary purposes behind using online technologies are to campaign and to fundraise, not to organise responses or to coordinate volunteer efforts. But as their efforts become more sophisticated, it seems likely that the Katrina response will start to look less like a one-off, and more like an early prototype.

Lead, follow, or get out of the way?

The success of the volunteer response to Katrina in allowing citizens to collaborate productively without help from the state begs a question: is it best for government to stay out of the way in such circumstances? The answer cannot be a straightforward 'yes' – Katrinalist is a powerful intervention, but voluntary efforts will always have their downsides.

The first drawback is – what happens if the volunteers get things wrong? They are, after all, not really accountable to anyone. While Michael Brown's failings meant that he could go from doing 'a helluva job' to not having a job at all, the organisers of the Katrinalist effort could not be fired by democratically accountable politicians or public servants.

And voluntary efforts will never be enough on their own – information sharing cannot simply supplant the emergency services. In the aftermath of a crime such as the 7/7 bombings in London, there was little that online volunteers could do. In such circumstances it is only right that the emergency services coordinate the response.

But despite the downsides, collaborative online responses to problems – both disasters like Hurricane Katrina and more mundane local concerns – are likely to increase in number and importance as a parallel system to those set up by governments. Politicians and public services will need to work out how to live with these innovations, and sometimes they will need to make the difficult decision to get out of the way and let citizens do their thing.

Paul Miller is a Demos Associate. Niamh Gallagher is a researcher at Demos.

Notes

1   S Berlin Johnson, 'Ordinary people can solve communication problems much quicker than clueless government officials when catastrophes like hurricane Katrina strike', *Discover* 26, no. 12 (Dec 2005), see www.discover.com/issues/dec-05/departments/emerging-technology/ (accessed 24 Jul 2006 and 10 Mar 2007).

2   Ibid.

3   www.smartmobs.com/archive/2005/09/09/katrina_peoplef.html (accessed 26 Jul 2006 and 10 Mar 2007).

4   J Surowiecki, *The Wisdom of Crowds: Why the many are smarter than the few and how collective wisdom shapes business, economies, societies and nations* (New York: Little, Brown, 2004).

5   http://meta.wikimedia.org/wiki/Benevolent_dictator (accessed 16 Feb 2007).

6   Y Benkler, *The Wealth of Networks* (Yale: Yale University Press, 2006).

7   Ibid.

8   www-128.ibm.com/developerworks/podcast/dwi/cm-int082206.txt (accessed 16 Feb 2007).

9   www.businessweek.com/mediacenter/podcasts/podcasting/jeff_jarvis20050908.htm (accessed 16 Feb 2007).

10 Ibid.

10. Policing the front line

Charlie Edwards

The notice board in Cowley police station is ablaze with posters advertising everything from free legal advice for young people to meeting dates for Alcoholics Anonymous. A poster offers free bicycles to people who have had theirs stolen.

The notice board is just one symptom of the major changes that have taken hold in the city as a new approach to police work takes hold. Neighbourhood policing relies heavily on partnerships between the police, communities, local businesses and other public services. The logic is simple – the police recognise that they can create safe communities only if they work with a wide variety of other public services, or as they are sometimes referred to, 'the extended police family'.

The word 'neighbourhood' is important here. Oxford City is divided into six devolved area committees that coordinate local services – each has its own area police commander as well as participation from local politicians and a broad spectrum of public service providers. Sitting beneath the committees are 22 neighbourhoods, each with its own police rating – 'priority', 'enhanced' or 'capable', depending on crime levels. A local policing board combining councillors and local people oversees the whole affair.

This case study focuses on three kinds of people who sit at the heart of the complex web of relationships underpinning neighbourhood policing: the first responder, the proactive manager and the system leader.

Working with the community

In the canteen of Cowley police station Sergeant Ian Uttley from Thames Valley Police is having an earnest conversation with one of Oxford's area commanders. In the past couple of weeks there has been an attempted murder on the Blackbird Leys estate, one of the largest council estates in Europe and one of the most deprived in England. This is a crucial time for Ian, who leads the neighbourhood policing team in Oxford City.

He needs his officers and police community support officers (PCSOs) on the street, reassuring neighbours nearby to the attack, picking up intelligence from conversations with local people and providing a presence on the estate during a period of instability. The problem, it becomes clear, is that it isn't going to be that simple. To begin with, the foiled terrorist plot in August of this year (aimed at bringing down aeroplanes across the Atlantic) has meant officers from Thames Valley Police have been seconded to the ongoing anti-terrorist operation in High Wycombe.

He also needs to have police officers on core response (think flashing blue lights), and finally some officers are on leave or off sick. All of which leaves Ian with only one officer to hand. Without his full compliment of police officers Ian has to rely on his wider network, not just PCSOs, but street wardens, council officers and members of the public who live and work on the estate. He will also rely on his own network of key individual contacts.

Key individual contacts are those people from a range of organisations that Ian works with on matters of neighbourhood policing. They are the people who will support him in his role, and who can rely on him to help them if and when they need.

A huge amount of effort goes into developing networks of key individual contacts. They are time-intensive, and because of changing shift patterns and operational matters difficult to maintain. Ian's frustration is that there is a lack of support for nurturing these important relationships, when their value seems so 'blindingly obvious'. Ian's network of key individual contacts is absolutely crucial for his role as a first responder.

The first responder

In his current position Ian, by his own admission, is able to 'get things done'. He was given responsibility for neighbourhood policing a year ago and while he has a set of priorities and objectives from higher up in Thames Valley Police, he is also driven by the needs of the community via the Neighbourhood Action Groups (NAG), which aim to bring together the police and a wide group of people and services from the community to identify the priorities for the locality.

NAGs identify three priorities for the local services to act on, for example noisy neighbours or abandoned cars. The groups have a three-month delivery cycle, with their work assessed by the local crime and disorder reduction partnership (CDRP),[1] which also provides most neighbourhood-level funding. That makes it important for Ian to ensure that he is meeting the aspirations of the local residents and meeting the priorities of the CDRP.

For Ian, devolving leadership down to his level is crucial if he is to have the freedom to help direct resources. In doing so Ian must balance the bureaucratic elements of his role with the more flexible approach that is needed when collaborating with local communities. As an example Ian mentions Mike, who works for Oxford City Council and is in charge of removing abandoned cars.

Abandoned cars have not necessarily been 'abandoned'. They may well be 'pooled cars' for use by a variety of people for any reason. Pooled cars are a neighbourhood nightmare. Some are road legal, but more often than not they are untaxed and have no licence. The keys tend to be left accessible for anyone 'in the know' to use.

Joy riders take them for a spin causing danger to other road users, arsonists see them as a potential bonfire display, while drug dealers frequently roam the city in them looking for their next sell. With one phone call to Mike, Ian can have the car taken away. The short conversation Ian has with Mike is a perfect example of how simple and effective collaboration at the front line can be.

But, however simple and effective collaboration might be, there are a number of organisational issues that Ian must contend with. To begin with, police forces put great emphasis on ensuring that best practice and learning is learnt across the force. So Ian must complete a basic audit of his conversation and any work that results from it. This seemingly protracted process is known as problem-oriented policing and has its roots in community policing in the United States.

While the process is time consuming, it does allow colleagues to gain an insight into how a problem is solved – something that is extremely important for the development of the force as a whole.

The proactive manager

There is barely any free space on the walls of Superintendent Jim Trotman's office. Sheets of paper outline current performance – graphs with multiple lines zigzag across posters, highlighting the current trends in crime detection, domestic violence, violent crime and crime reduction. The British Crime Survey target performance chart and the Local Police Area's performance targets hang on the wall behind his desk.

Jim is all for loose structures which allow dynamism at the front line. But, he admits, the current structure of the police hampers some forms of collaboration, while policing targets don't capture the 'non-target-specific' work that makes up a lot of neighbourhood policing. How to measure the process of building the kind of close relationships with local communities that lead to a greater sense of safety and security?

Jim recently moved from West Berkshire to Oxford City to take up the role of Local Police Area (LPA) Commander, with an emphasis on neighbourhood policing. But Jim might be better described as one of several proactive managers that supervise community safety.

Proactive managers play a crucial role in neighbourhood policing. They must focus on maximising collaborative approaches across a spectrum of local services at the same time as meeting targets imposed from above. In order for this to work in practice, Jim must take a holistic view of community safety management, and be able to negotiate between the political, bureaucratic and public spaces. But this cannot happen without the support of others.

The system leader

Collaboration between local services in Oxford City is slowly taking shape – thanks in no small part to Richard Adams, the community safety officer for the city. Richard works with the full range of council services, local businesses and the public, not to mention the police and NAGs. Richard could be described as a system leader.

Pinned to the notice board in the meeting room is a piece of paper with a list of values that senior directors in the council must adhere to: Openness, Trust, Respect and Integrity – values that could just as well be the basis for collaboration, as without all of them in place collaborative approaches will fail. Like Jim, Richard believes that looser structures aid collaboration and should be developed from the bottom up, with the support of a top-down approach by managers.

The slow pace of collaborative initiatives is, he says, a product of the traditional siloed mentality of public service. One way of speeding things up might involve the city council in tackling some of the barriers it imposes, including a re-examination of its reporting lines, its focus on individual and service targets and the ever-present tension between what local communities want and the funding the council can obtain from central government.

Richard believes that greater collaboration will emerge over time, but he is acutely aware of the need to have the right systems in place to allow it to mature and the need to develop the skills that are required to ensure it is sustainable. As we have seen, collaboration between local services on the front line can make a huge difference to communities in both the city centre and the Blackbird Leys estate. But collaboration cannot work in a vacuum. It needs some sort of structure, albeit a loose one, and a mix of the right personalities and support to ensure its success.

Skills for collaboration

In order for collaboration to be a success, police and council officers, caseworkers and others need to have the right skill sets to develop new relationships, sustain them and utilise them. From Richard's anecdotal evidence there is clearly some way to go.

People skills in particular are critical, but often underdeveloped. Being too overbearing can end any collaborative venture, while a lack of enthusiasm can mean collaboration never gets off the ground. So Richard argues that public servants need more help to develop their skills and networks.

And people sometimes struggle to see the incentives for collaboration – which are often hidden and sometimes cannot be exploited by any one individual. Collaboration is doomed if too many people dismiss it as a gimmick, resist working outside their comfort zone, or jealously guard their own networks.

Richard highlights an example from his work in neighbourhood policing. A 'priority' neighbourhood can have up to five wardens (paid for by the council) between four and six PCSOs (half funded by the council and police) and a police sergeant and up to five constables. Richard believes that given the space and, most importantly, the go ahead, collaboration between wardens and constables as well as the wider community could happen. Yet somehow, that kind of joint working has not become as widespread as he had expected. What could be a win–win situation for those involved ultimately ends up with the public losing out.

Richard believes that to make collaboration happen on a more regular and sustainable basis a system needs to be designed that allows individuals to take a broader view of their work and gives them the freedom to move beyond the traditional boundaries of their service. Richard qualifies this by suggesting that any change needs to have a light touch – it shouldn't be about formal structure.

Towards flexible structures?

The Crime and Disorder Act 1998 placed a legal obligation on all local authorities and police to jointly develop and implement a strategy for tackling crime and disorder. As the priorities for Oxford City have changed and expanded to encompass new priorities, so the structure of the partnership has evolved too.

An important element in this process has been striking the right balance between creating more bureaucratic processes (such as complex audit trails and more partnership meetings) and focusing on empowering those individuals on the front line to work across the different services to make a difference. As one interviewee pointed out: '90 per cent of the work will be done outside the Town Hall not in it.'

But there are a number of obstacles to getting the balance right, not least the way that community safety is funded. Oxford's Safer Community Partnership is one major funding route controlled and evaluated by central government, through the Government Office of South East England (GOSE). Thames Valley Police negotiate, then sign up to crime reduction targets that unlock the budget.

GOSE measures crime across the south east using recorded crime data and the British Crime Survey, which together provide a fairly reliable indication of crime. However, there are still irregularities in the system which mean, for example, that while the British Crime Survey shows bulk crime (ie cycle theft in Oxford City) as being a major issue, the real concern to most of Oxford is drug abuse and violent robbery.

The top-down approach to targeting crime can clearly be ineffective, and it raises real issues of accountability too. No one seems to remember when the crime reduction officer for GOSE was last hauled before the public. As such, the system lacks credibility with the police and council officers, while leaving communities wondering why their services appear disjointed.

Collaboration is the future but . . .

Unlike formal partnerships, collaboration is messy, complicated and to a great extent based on individual relationships. In a world of targets and metrics that must demonstrate effectiveness collaboration can end up the loser – 'the final thing in my in-tray'.

No one has yet come up with a system for measuring collaboration – how can you demonstrate on a graph the importance of meeting four members of the council? Yet as Ian and his colleagues prove, it can be the life blood of good community service. Collaboration will mean an abandoned car is removed from across the street; a case worker will visit a neighbour about anti-social behaviour, or an environmental issue will be dealt with. Collaboration gets things done.

In an increasingly complex environment, collaboration allows public services on the front line to negotiate the bureaucratic partnership models that so often lead to inertia. The danger is that, when they do so, frontline staff are faced with audit trail and accountability mechanisms that mean positive acts of collaboration are rewarded with days of form filling.

Collaboration is also hampered by the simple realities of policing in the twenty-first century – priorities from above can shift much needed resources to other initiatives, and explaining that you need an hour off to engage with contacts in your network can be frowned on when there are urgent priorities to meet.

Tapping into collaboration

Richard is excited about community engagement – primarily because he knows that the people he serves have got the answers to their problems. They are, he believes, 'a huge untapped source' – but at the moment neither the police nor the council wardens nor the various structures in place have been able to tap into this energy. Collaborating with citizens, he says, is the real aim and everyone knows this.

One initiative that has been mooted by Liberal Democrat councillors is the introduction of Neighbourhood Environment Action Teams. The proposal sounds a NEAT idea for further collaboration, bringing the wide array of council services and police and communities ever closer together and builds on a range of initiatives like the environment audit, which are undertaken by neighbourhood teams to assess the visible 'incivilities' of their area and record them for a 'before and after' comparison.

It is hoped that the NEAT teams will play a key part in tackling a wide range of environmental and anti-social behaviour problems including refuse collection, street cleansing, recycling, parks and open spaces, abandoned vehicles, fly tipping, dog fouling and graffiti. However, the success of NEATs will depend on their ability to manage relationships across council services and create an environment in which further collaboration can occur.

Collaboration is happening in Oxford – but it has yet to realise its full transformative potential. For that to happen, local public services need to be bold enough to take a giant step into the unknown and radically shift responsibility away from managers in the town hall to frontline staff. Combine that with command and control systems that recognise the importance of local priorities over national targets, and Oxford's police can create a system in which they daily cross institutional boundaries and work together in new and exciting ways.

Thank you to Sergeant Ian Uttley, Superintendent Jim Trotman, Inspector Stan Gilmour and Chief Inspector Russ Wootton (all Thames Valley Police); and Councillor Caroline Van Zyl and Richard Adams (Oxford City Council).

Charlie Edwards is a Demos researcher.

Notes

1   Known locally as the Oxford City Safer Partnership.

11. New leadership for the collaborative state

Valerie Hannon

Sometimes, a phrase or a conversation sticks in the memory, seeming to capture something of its time. Around 1995, when I was the director of education in a large English county, one of the secondary head teachers in the local education authority remarked sharply: 'My only concern and thought must be: what is going to make for the very best for my school? If you can't understand that, we have very little to talk about.'

We did, as it happened, have a good deal more to talk about. But the remark captures for me the spirit of that period, which has been more or less transformed in this last decade. I do not think it would now be acceptable, in polite company, for a school leader to take such a stance.

The commonly held, professionally respectable approach of most school leaders in the new century is to acknowledge the interconnectedness of their actions. To a greater or lesser extent, they accept the implications of what they do – in, say, exclusions and admissions – for other schools. One is much more likely to hear school leaders aspire to take on the responsibility for all the learners in their local area.

But while considerable strides have been made in that direction, there are still a lot of road blocks. This essay describes some of those road blocks, sets out why innovative approaches to leadership are needed in such a context, and describes the ongoing work of some public service innovators to shape new models.

The rise of partnership and collaboration between schools

It is interesting that, despite a range of policies that would appear to steer the system towards competition and an inward focus, the evidence is that the majority of schools are now engaged in meaningful inter-school collaboration.

They might be a part of one or more of any number of funded programmes: primary strategy learning networks, education improvement partnerships or leading edge partnerships, to name but a few. Or they might be a part of a locally grown, unfunded collaborative network. And an increasing number have taken these developments to the next, more formal level of creating a federation – involving some degree of cooperation or integration of governance structures.

Our work with schools and school leaders deeply engaged in developing their services in these ways has, however, started to reveal some tensions and fault lines. Reference has already been made to some of the conflicting pressures. Funding follows enrolments and there is over-provision of places; league tables profile the 'performance' of individual schools (irrespective of the part other schools may have played in the learners' successes); Ofsted inspections continue to be conducted only on individual schools.

Collaboration also has its own set of internal challenges and tensions. These include in particular the problem of sustainability. Collaboration built – as it frequently is – on strong trusting personal relationships is necessarily going to be at risk when key individuals move on. Connected to this is the degree to which governing bodies are all too often somewhat detached from the practice of their school's collaborative work.

With all these pressures pulling in the opposite direction, it is remarkable that the collaborative movement has thrived to the degree which it undoubtedly has. I believe that this is because of the imperative for professional educators to collaborate, which never died: instead, it persisted, but became more difficult to express.

Additionally, a new generation of policies, and rising aspirations for learners, have placed a premium on effective collaboration. The publication of *Every Child Matters*,[1] identifying five key outcomes for every learner, is predicated on the understanding that only multi-agency and inter-school working of a quality never realised before will be capable of delivering these outcomes.

It has resulted in the biggest change in local governance since the 1944 Act: the 'local education authority' has disappeared, and integrated Children's Services departments have replaced them.

No such easy re-organisational solutions are available at the school level. New ways of working need to emerge. Similarly, the expectation that all 14–19-year-olds will be entitled to access to a much broader range of courses and opportunities than any single secondary school can hope to deliver, carries a similar implication. Sustainable, effective and efficient collaboration therefore has been well and truly incorporated into the policy pantheon.

The knowledge base around effective school-to-school collaboration is extensive and continues to grow. What has become apparent, however, is that there is a missing dimension, which is the new forms and models of leadership to support these developments. It is insufficient to produce mere lists of the kinds of characteristics of the leaders currently playing these roles – we also need a deeper understanding of the practice and ways of embedding it.

It is not coincidental that, simultaneously, the old models of school leadership are subject to increasing pressures from other directions. There are a number of reasons why schools, local authorities and the government are looking to evolve new forms of leadership and governance:

- ○ to support a school or schools 'causing concern'
- ○ to spread high-quality leadership across schools and deploy it more effectively
- ○ to overcome falling rolls linked to rural isolation while maintaining the quality of teaching and learning

O   to deliver all-age learning
O   to resolve issues around headteacher appointment or
      succession: how is excellent leadership in all 18,000
      primary schools to be secured, for example, in the face of
      the expected retirement of 40 per cent of primary heads
      in the next seven years?
O   to develop services, such as early years, special needs or
      community-based learning in radically new 'customer-
      focused' forms, which might lead to the integration of
      existing institutions into 'learning centres' serving
      children, young people, their parents and other adults.

Taken together, these are compelling reasons to devote focused
capacity to developing leadership models explicitly designed to
facilitate solutions to these challenges.

'Next Practice' in leadership for collaboration

The Innovation Unit[2] was established in 2002 to promote
practitioner-led innovation. It has focused its work since 2005 on the
concept of developing 'Next Practice' – looking at entirely new
approaches as distinct from transferring or disseminating
acknowledged 'best' or 'good' practice. It has done this by means of a
methodology centred on releasing practitioner and user creativity.[3]

This methodology is being employed across a range of content
areas. The first of these addresses the challenges which have been
identified in the first part of the essay: it is devoted to encouraging
schools to developing models of leadership which more adequately
meet their needs and aspirations: specifically system leadership –
defined as 'leadership beyond a single institution'.

Since this is an evolving practice and theory, it is premature to offer
tightly bounded definitions. However, some clear characteristics are
emerging. System leaders are those teachers and heads who are
capable of managing networks that cross institutional boundaries in
order to: share resources, coordinate effort, and maximise the impact
of several educational institutions on their local area. Through this

contribution to local solutions, they are able to influence and co-create policy for the system as a whole.

This fits well with Michael Fullan's definition of 'a very different model of leadership from the traditional single school model – one that is extended beyond the school, highly interactive horizontally and vertically, and engaged in communication and critique of policies and strategies'.[4]

Unless better models of system leadership can be developed, it is unlikely that the forms of collaboration between schools which are so urgently needed will flourish or be sustained.

It is fundamental to this approach that the problems – and solutions – should be those of the schools themselves, rather than being identified by others, be they academics, policy thinkers or theorists. The Innovation Unit therefore identified schools and local systems which were already pushing at the boundaries of current leadership, governance and accountability structures.

The Next Practice project on system leadership, which is being run in partnership with the National College for School Leadership (NCSL), has identified 16 'field trial' sites, comprising collaborations of various types. It will support, challenge and assist in the development of their thinking and practice over the period September 2006 to March 2008.

The project will also work closely with a much wider community of interest (comprising both other sites from which the 16 were chosen and other schools engaged in similar innovative work). This community of practice will connect with the work through the best developed knowledge management techniques, actual and virtual. The power of this work must extend well beyond the 16 field trials themselves. And it will extend also beyond their successes, for it is likely that – as in most innovation – powerful learning will be had from failures as well as successes.

The following cases studies have been selected from the group of field trials which are working with the IU and the NCSL to develop new models of leadership. The first, Darlington Education Village, is taking the focus of the five outcomes set out in *Every Child Matters*

(ECM)[5] as the guiding principle for the creation of new system leadership.

Darlington Education Village

Darlington Education Village is a 2–19 federation of three schools: a special school, a primary school and a community secondary school. It has been developing over the past four years, and moved into stunning new buildings on a single site in 2006. The federation has a strong focus on community leadership and engagement and adopted its 'Village' title for its reference to the proverb that 'it takes a whole village to raise a child'. This commitment to the ideal of 'everyone watching out for each other' is given symbolic expression by the positioning of the special school at the centre of the village, not on its margins.

The federation's current focus is on building capacity for system leadership in order, as they put it, to 'bring ECM to life'. In September 2005, they established a single governing body with an unusual structure. Its four committees (for teaching and learning, inclusion, community and village support and resources) are designed to link directly to the delivery of the five outcomes of the ECM agenda.

The leadership of the federation is currently at a transitional stage. The respective headteachers of the schools are still in place, but the federation is in the process of implementing a radically new 'whole village' leadership structure. The structure continues to reflect the priorities of ECM: beneath an executive director, five other directors will assume responsibility for delivering the five outcomes, in conjunction with other services. When implemented, these developments will have the potential to make a real difference to provision and outcomes for young people in Darlington and are also likely to influence national debates on federations and partnerships, and on all-through schools. If successful, the local authority would like to use the village as a template for shaping educational provision for the rest of Darlington.

The challenge of delivering ambitious new opportunities for learners in the 14–19 age group has been referred to. To design this provision, and put in place the arrangements to realise it, is in itself a tough assignment. How though, are these arrangements to be made sustainable over time, and how can leadership facilitate this? A number of the system leadership field trials are addressing this issue. The case study of Stevenage demonstrates one approach.

Stevenage partnership

The first of this country's new towns, Stevenage has experienced considerable change over the last two decades. The employment infrastructure has deteriorated, with a commensurate impact on potential vocational pathways for young people. The schools in Stevenage all share common problems related to the delivery of a post-16 provision, along with the wider challenges of size viability and the need to raise achievement levels. Grappling with similar concerns, schools in the area have forged a powerful voluntary alliance – partly out of necessity, and partly because they believe that working collaboratively is the only way to successfully deliver a 14–19 entitlement.

All the 11–19 community schools in Stevenage, along with the two special schools, the pupil referral unit and the further education college, have formed a partnership to deliver 14–19 provision to the town. The partnership is led by a 14–19 director (previously a headteacher of one of the schools) and has so far had local authority support and national support, too, through a 'Pathfinder' programme. The alliance has a base in a central business park and has developed materials to support the work and an infrastructure of practices that is impressive. They plan to take this work further under the aspirational umbrella of 'Stevenage: A Learning Town'. Their Next Practice field trial will create a small governance group designed to bridge the gap between sectors. The group will be directly accountable for the configuration of provision, which will include town-wide curriculum planning and joint blocked timetables.

In an important sense, the innovators profiled in this essay are all struggling with the same dilemma. In a highly devolved system, where the impetus remains strong to locate more power to local communities, how can a strategic approach be maintained so that the dividends of collaboration are fully exploited and sustained? New forms of leadership must be part of the solution – and that concept of 'leadership' needs to be holistic, incorporating new approaches to governance also. Knowsley, on Merseyside, is proposing to innovate in this field through federated governance structures for secondary provision across the entire borough.

Continuous improvement in Knowsley

The local authority of Knowsley, the third most deprived in the country, has earned a justifiable reputation for innovative and groundbreaking approaches to school improvement based on developing partnerships between the authority and schools. Over the past five years, it has become skilled at effecting positive change through collaboration, securing substantial improvements in secondary standards (doubling the percentage getting five A* to C GCSEs to 47.8 per cent). Wanting to continue to develop a high quality of service, Knowsley found itself pushing against the limits of what the existing system will deliver.

Knowsley believes that continuous improvement is rooted in a co-leadership approach. Its intention is radically to transform leadership and governance arrangements as part of a complete overhaul of the education system across the borough. It will be closing all secondary schools and, using funding from the Building Schools for the Future programme, opening eight new Learning Centres, which it intends to combine into a federated structure. It is also beginning to think about how primary schools could be incorporated into this arrangement.

Knowsley's vision is for the implementation of a radical federated governance model, which secures collective ownership and accountability across the borough, and also dovetails with the delivery of wider public services. The broader context for these proposals is a radical plan for neighbourhood and community regeneration. 'Concept Knowsley' will tackle the areas of greatest deprivation in the borough and ensure delivery of a consistent quality of services in all areas. A successful Next Practice field trial for Knowsley would establish a robust, secure and continually developing system of governance for children, young people and their families that would be a key pillar of local regeneration. And this would provide a powerful model with resonance for many other localities struggling with similarly intractable problems.

Conclusion: new leadership, new skills

As the innovators in these field trials seek to drive forward purposive collaboration focused on outcomes for users, we will learn a great deal about how leadership itself needs to evolve. We will have to revisit our notions of what is needed in the governance of schools and other services, and how these can draw much more directly on local capacities. 'System leaders' will not always be drawn from the ranks of teachers. As we see an exponential growth in the demand for more personalised services, alongside new market opportunities, we should expect to see new combinations of services taking shape. Their leaders will be those who are developing new skill sets: closely attentive to the target community, collaborative by instinct and practice, and outcome driven. For some, the transformation has already begun.

Valerie Hannon is director of The Innovation Unit.

Notes

1   Department for Education and Skills, *Every Child Matters* (London: DfES, 2005).
2   See The Innovation Unit website at www.innovation-unit.co.uk/ (accessed 10 Mar 2007).
3   See 'Next Practice' on IU website at www.innovation-unit.co.uk/index.php?option=com_content&task=section&id=3&Itemid=101 (accessed 10 Mar 2007).
4   M Fullan, *System Thinkers in Action* (Nottingham: The Innovation Unit/DfES Publications, 2004).
5   The five 'outcomes for children' defined by *Every Child Matters* are to be healthy, stay safe, enjoy and achieve, make a positive contribution, and achieve economic wellbeing.

vercoming the
idden barriers

Henry Tam

Asking people to collaborate better to promote the public good – within the public sector and with the private and voluntary sectors as well – is now, more than ever, the mantra of reform programmes. There is no shortage of case studies or management theories on how collaboration can be strengthened to deliver more efficient and effective services for the public we serve. Instead of adding to this wealth of literature, a good selection of which is included in this Demos collection, I would like to focus my contribution on some of the hidden barriers to the development of a truly collaborative state, and suggest how these can be overcome through a variety of culture change initiatives.

In my 20 years in public service, I have been involved in leading a wide range of collaborative projects covering many different policy areas. From the successes and the setbacks I have experienced, I can discern a number of common barriers often shielded from critical exposure. There are many effective routes to collaborative working, yet none of them can be relied on if these barriers get in the way. It is useful to encourage public servants to adopt good practices in advancing collaboration, but ultimately we must also face up to the factors that block progress.

Routes to collaboration

I will begin by looking at a number of successful collaborative ventures. At Lewisham, in 1988 we created the first branded discount card, which entitled both those who qualified for concessions because they were unemployed, old age pensioners, students etc, and those who paid a lump sum membership fee, to free or discounted use of a wide range of leisure facilities provided by the Council and numerous private sector venues. The Vantage Card removed the stigma associated with conventional 'concessionary passes' for people on low income, and helped to attract more people from all socioeconomic backgrounds to use the facilities on offer. The key challenge was to bring service providers across the public and private sectors together to back the common objectives of the scheme and collaborate in marketing it. Despite the initial scepticism, more within the public sector itself than with private sector partners, the growth of bilateral deals reached a tipping point where participation became the norm, and the Vantage Card offer became widely known and used in the catchment area.

If generating returns from a common arrangement was a key factor in the Vantage Card collaboration, another of my examples had no such ingredient. I first met the people who were to form the core of the Haverhill Regeneration Partnership in 1994 when I agreed to help them pull together a bid to the Single Regeneration Budget. The bid failed. In the course of preparing the bid, however, we had brought together a group of highly dedicated residents, old and young, statutory body representatives, voluntary organisations and local businesses, who discovered they shared a determination to improve the quality of life of their town lying – some said marginalised – on the borders of Essex, Cambridgeshire and Suffolk.

They had deprivation problems, but these were not as serious as those in inner London or some of the coastal towns. They decided not to stress the problems in their town in order to bid for deprivation-based funding, but to focus on the opportunities for improvement. I agreed to chair the partnership which succeeded in bringing in support and investment from a range of public and private sources, all impressed by the readiness of those involved in the partnership to collaborate to build a better Haverhill. It is tempting to say that even though the Haverhill Partnership did not get the initial funding it sought, its members had something powerfully in common – their shared vision for a better town – to drive collaborative working.

But in the absence of any such common bond, I found it equally feasible to establish in the late 1990s a collaborative group when most had predicted it would be impossible. The group was COVER (Community and Voluntary sector forum: Eastern Region). In the light of the government's emerging regional policies, I met voluntary and community organisations across the East of England to discuss the need to develop a transparent and effective forum to enable voluntary and community sector (VCS) organisations to form and articulate their shared views to regional public institutions.

But regional policy development was often remote from most people's concerns, and the great majority of VCS groups in the region either saw each other as distant relations with little in common or competitors for funding. When it was pointed out to them the alternative of remaining fragmented without a regional voice when others would speak in their name without any accountability, they began to consider the implications and gradually support emerged that enabled me to work with a steering group to form COVER. COVER went on to elect its own chair and executive committee and become one of the most successful regional umbrella organisations in the country.

In the last six or seven years, I have been involved in the development of other collaborative projects on a regional and national level in support of crime reduction, offender management, health improvement, regeneration and cultural activities. The most recent has been the government's 'Together We Can' campaign, which brought together 12 government departments, local authorities and community sector organisations to press for more effective empowerment of citizens in shaping public policies and services. The production of a shared action plan alone had persuaded many that despite the entrenched silos, collaboration could still play its part. Those who contributed to the action plan were not looking from the outset for a joint enterprise, but came round to the view that they could advance their own agenda more forcefully through being a part of a larger scale, higher profile exercise.

Barriers to replicating collaborative success

From the examples cited, you might argue that, although the relationship between the potential players can vary, as long as you can persuade each party to see that collaboration allows them to achieve something they would not have otherwise attained, then the rest is just a matter of sharpening the skills of joint working.

If that was the case, then we might expect to see a lot more successful collaborative work. In reality, it is not the apparent ingredients behind our success stories – people drawn into a set of common aims they can relate to, constant investment in facilitating shared understanding, trust built up from practical cooperation, and leadership to maintain focus and drive progress – that hold the key to their replication. It is much more about their ability to form a collaborative dynamic because a number of critical barriers have been avoided or overcome.

For every success story of collaboration, I can point to problems and frustration where the players involved were just as conscious of what they could achieve together, but the joint enterprise came to a halt because one or more of the barriers to collaboration had made progress impossible. Without going directly into the sensitive territories of reviewing these cases, we can nonetheless consider the key lessons from them by examining the generic features of these barriers. I will outline these under the following headings:

o   the imperial court syndrome
o   the pseudo-diversity trap
o   the innovations-first/citizens-last complex
o   the postmodern feudal barons.

The imperial court syndrome

All public services operate under chains of command which lead inevitably upward to a central power structure. In practice, not everything is determined by those at the highest level. To keep the complex machinery of government going, the majority of decisions have to be delegated down the line. Where the good sense of subsidiarity prevails, this delegation would always travel down to the lowest possible level where decisions can be made effectively in direct response to those affected by them. However, between the issues which need the closest attention of those at the top of the state power system and those which are left to those best placed to deal with them lower down the hierarchy, there are in different parts of the system policy matters which, for reasons of media attention or personal interest, at times get pulled up the line for detailed consideration. For example, a number of public services may be discussing with people in certain parts of the country how they can come to feel more confident that something will be done to reverse the decline of their quality of life. As soon as a distant part of the command chain (ie those who are quite a few steps above the decision-makers involved with the issue, though they may not be at the very top themselves) declares its interest (and control) in the matter, the prospect of a serious barrier looms.

While it is perfectly legitimate for anyone in the command chain to take an interest in how an issue down the line is being resolved, it can sometimes be difficult to pull back from positioning oneself as the key problem-solver. This tendency for some high up the command chain to make it their in-tray business to deal with what is very much below their pay grade has all too common negative consequences for would-be collaborators down the line. Like all those who, while occupying prestigious positions in old imperial courts, could not resist showing their prowess for resolving problems in distant parts of the empire, they issued edicts without being able to devote sufficient time to study the intricacies of the problem. Whatever those willing collaborators down the line have managed to develop as a way forward, distant instructions steer them into an ever-decreasing circle, with messages made more obscure through each iterative interpretation by each successive transmitter. No one in close contact with the issues can get to talk them through with the one who has taken charge. And in the end, the problem is shelved because no one can find a way to satisfy the distant decision-maker while still dealing with the real issues before them.

Of course it does not have to be like that. Many senior decision-makers know the value of applying themselves to where they are needed, and give their trust and support to those down their respective command chains to develop collaborative solutions for other problems. But those who do not are in desperate need for some help with understanding why they should change their approach.

The pseudo-diversity trap

It is commonplace these days to be told that people from different organisations, different sectors, indeed ordinary citizens with different backgrounds, are sought to build new collaborative arrangements. Where the embrace of diversity is genuine it is undoubtedly a huge boost to collaborative working as people can stop worrying about how their distinct backgrounds may hold them back and concentrate on working with others on equal terms. Where diversity is not fully embraced, people need to set energy aside to build bridges and create a more unifying environment. However, the worst-case scenario is when the pseudo-diversity trap is laid. This happens when the dominant culture proclaims its commitment to bringing people from diverse backgrounds together and cites the variety of organisational, gender and racial characteristics of those who feature in their teams. But beneath the superficial diversity of appearances lies the core prototype of the assertive individual – male or female, black or white. The expectation is that effective participants will exhibit the resolute confidence to talk the talk of 'hard edge' outcomes and unhesitatingly predict trajectories towards success, even when the complexities of the problems in question render such an approach unworkable.

People recruited as lay members to public bodies to give a 'citizen perspective' have most often found this kind of pseudo-diversity stifling. They put themselves forward on the understanding that they would be welcome as integral players, but soon discover that they are marginalised for not being able to come up with tough, robust expressions of sharp ideas. The same applies to people already in the public sector but who do not conform to the core prototype. Their preference for listening, reflection, consensus building with the wider public is viewed as a propensity to excessive caution, when the group should be surging forward with a rapidly defined goal. Any attempt to build collaboration which excludes women and ethnic minorities will be very swiftly exposed and challenged. But the pseudo-diversity trap leaves people feeling that it is they who do not match up to the standards required, and they withdraw rather than demand a change of culture. For more collaborative arrangements to work in the public sector, serious efforts will have to be made to target pseudo-diversity traps, and strengthen the confidence, especially of community participants, in being themselves in helping to take the shared project forward.

The innovations-first/citizens-last complex

Innovations have a vital part to play in the public sector. We cannot unthinkingly stick with the same practices and ignore opportunities for improvements. But to fixate exclusively on innovations and dismiss every established method of meeting people's needs as 'old hat' is immensely damaging. Public service collaborations tend to work well when those involved share the experience of enhancing the quality of life of the citizens they serve. Yet when the demand for innovative practices trumps the actual needs of citizens, the public service ethos is turned upside down. Instead of channelling resources, for example, to what would make the biggest difference when there is a queue of tried and tested initiatives waiting for funding support, potential collaborators have to come up with something completely different, and the funds are diverted to a continuous stream of new projects.

Even when some of the new ideas turn out to have a significant impact, collaborators cannot concentrate on bedding down the new practices, which is essential for them to take hold. Instead, the expectation of being able to present yet another new initiative diverts those involved from building any lasting relationship with the citizens they are meant to serve, and moves them to coming up with yet more innovations. In the private sector, a successful product is branded to give it lasting appeal and nurtured to prolong its efficacy. In the public sector, all too often branding is regarded as a short-term mechanism to grab some media attention before quickly moving on to something else.

The postmodern feudal barons

Take any collaborative project. If those involved work for public service leaders who value cooperation, they will be able to move forward confidently and productively without looking over their shoulder all the time. But if they were under postmodern feudal barons (PFBs), who present themselves as the most forward-thinking, radical, can-do executives – when their deepest inclination is to proclaim their own achievements in their own domain – then the chance of success is much diminished. PFBs live by the boundaries which delineate their jurisdiction. Beyond those boundaries, they have no interest as to how their actions might help or hinder others. Within their own domain, they do not want the credit of any success to be shared with others. They, and they alone, deliver real achievements.

One can try to negotiate with PFBs to get them on board, but what one gets is still a precarious partnership, unlike those sustained by a genuine bond of common purpose. Furthermore PFBs do not accept shared responsibility for setbacks. At all times, they must be seen as the knights who can ride to the rescue of others, and never the other way round. The structure of delivery targets has in the past encouraged the rise of PFBs, because it demands individual ownership of complex delivery outcomes. Structures for performance assessment can of course be changed. And a shift towards team ownership of performance improvement would be one small, but important, step towards re-orienting the outlooks of PFBs. Another would be to alter their job descriptions to require cooperative working with others.

Conclusion

The barriers to collaboration I have considered are hidden because people tend to feel uncomfortable facing up to them. Many understandably feel that it would be better to placate those interfering from on high than to talk plainly about what really needs to be done. After all, one's career is at stake. The pseudo-diversity traps leave outsiders in no doubt that they have no long-term future and gives them little scope to challenge their cultural narrowness. And in the public sector where innovation is everything, it would take a brave person to say that the obsessive insistence on the new is getting in the way of delivering improvements for those we serve. As for the postmodern feudal barons, these are often one's boss or in a position to make one's boss feel uncomfortable, if one crosses the line.

This is not to say they are insurmountable. Putting the spotlight on previously hidden barriers is one way to start the process of removing them. It would take many more people, though, to speak out and create a climate wherein people in public service, especially those in powerful positions, are inclined to challenge these barriers and make it a part of a wider culture for collaboration to do away with them.

Henry Tam is deputy director of local democracy at the Department of Communities and Local Government. The views expressed in this article are put forward to stimulate discussion and are not to be taken as government policies.

Redesigning the system

13. Beyond delivery

A collaborative Whitehall
Simon Parker

Ask frontline public servants what stops them from collaborating and the same answer is likely to come back with depressing regularity: central government departments. Ministries get the blame for setting targets and budgets that might make sense on the national political stage, but get in the way of meeting local needs. Nationally accountable quangos fail to join up with locally accountable public servants. Local government's room to lead collaboration is hamstrung by a lack of budgetary and administrative discretion.

A more collaborative state does seem to demand a more collaborative kind of Whitehall – confused and contradictory central policy can easily become an almost insurmountable barrier to change at the local level. And yet the central policy apparatus of the state is one of the least reformed public services of the Blair years. In the era of the 'new localism' it remains all too easy to caricature departments as the lumbering relics of an antiquated management system. How can they possibly capture and deal with the sheer variety and complexity of the social problems facing places as different as Lewisham, Luton and Oxford? Even where the government has a clear outcome that it wants to meet, for instance reducing child poverty, the means of doing so is likely to vary according to local circumstances.

The truth is that Whitehall is feeling the strain of a long period of deep structural change in the way the UK runs its public services. A senior civil service that once prided itself on the quality of its policy advice is increasingly being asked to 'deliver' results for the government. This is not a bad aspiration. When Labour came to power its key goal was to improve public service standards quickly and predictably. The current set of tools government uses – from legislation to inspection and incentives to contracts – was the right one to force down waiting lists and drive up short-term performance.

But after a decade of that approach, government is still struggling to solve many of the really big problems that Britain faces. Simply raising the output of the UK's hospitals was not enough. Public services also need to get better at helping British children lead better lives, to create a population that is healthier and to help manage the tensions thrown up by our increasingly diverse society. Today, 'delivery' is less about providing more hospital operations and more about solving complex, multi-causal problems in collaboration with the people who face them. There are no easy answers to those problems, and addressing them requires joined-up solutions that are developed and implemented in partnership with the people they affect.

The public service reform debate is beginning to recognise that fact. Power is beginning to shift to the local level – not just to councils, but to increasingly assertive schools, foundation trusts and colleges that are close to people and the sources of problems. These developments are starting to highlight the fact that most senior civil servants do not actually deliver very much at all, at least not directly. They are more like system leaders, or perhaps 'collaborators-in-chief', trying to guide and influence large numbers of organisations that actually do deliver education and cleaner streets.

But this implies a major shift in the techniques civil servants use to create change. If the traditional models of governing are becoming less powerful, then governments need to explore new methods that do not so much seek to deliver things, as to determine goals and direction, provide resources and broker relationships that allow others to do their jobs. To lead whole systems of public service provision, central government departments themselves need to become more collaborative, encouraging department to work with department, but also connecting civil servants more effectively to the outside world of delivery.

This is not a simple managerial challenge that can be solved by the development of more professional market-management and procurement skills. It is also, critically, an opportunity to radically open up the civil service, involving a wider range of players in collaborative policy-making and collapsing the divide between policy and practice by bringing practitioners into the heart of the system.

This essay uses case studies of innovative work in Finland and New Zealand to argue that the traditional toolbox of government needs to be expanded. Techniques based on forcing and incentivising change need to be supplemented by a greater capacity to focus whole systems on government goals, and to augment and guide the work of existing organisations, rather than inventing major new policies and institutions every time a change is required.

We've been here before

Of course, this is not the first time anyone has suggested greater Whitehall integration – take Churchill's 'overlord' ministers of the early 1950s, Heath's central policy review staff, Blair's white paper *Modernising Government*[1] and his clusters of central strategy, anti-social behaviour or public service reform units. But most of these initiatives have simply involved strengthening the very centre of government – generally the Cabinet Office or particular politicians – to take an overview of a particular policy problem. They have never really addressed the underlying logic of Whitehall, challenging its siloed departmental structure or pushing policy-makers to work more effectively with the outside world.

Blair's central units seem ultimately to have had only limited success because they were unable to gain real influence in the great departments of state. The Social Exclusion Unit, for instance, was recently scaled down because its reports were felt to be having a decreasing impact after its move from the Cabinet Office to the Department for Communities and Local Government (DCLG). The unit has been reconstituted as a small taskforce with a remit to better embed its work in relevant government departments – health, education and the DCLG.[2]

Many of the reasons for this are obvious. Like most large public service organisations, the civil service is structured around functional boundaries with their own hierarchies and career structures. The organisations thus created all too easily become mildly competitive fiefdoms that sometimes resist connecting with the outside world.

This is compounded by the closed relationship between civil servants and ministers, which has had the effect of screening the centre of government off from robust external challenge. Until recently few people other than politicians really knew how departments were performing and only ministers had the power to change things. But short tenures mean that few cabinet members have the time or energy to reform their delivery machine except through big bang restructurings. The situation is not good for civil servants either – in the past they have often risked looking upward to the minister and not outward to the world they seek to change.

The closed nature of the civil service system helps to explain why much of the energy directed at joining up government over the past few years has been aimed at the local level. Real needs, people and places seem a more logical place to focus collaborative efforts than the more abstract business of preparing a white paper, while sheer proximity to problems can help to focus multiple organisations on solutions. Some of the pioneering attempts at local reform have been showcased in this collection – crime and disorder reduction partnerships, local strategic partnerships, networked learning communities.

But if problems are increasingly to be solved through collaboration on the ground, then what role can a more collaborative Whitehall play in supporting change and meeting ministerial goals? There are at least four roles it can assume:

o   *Incentivise:* Governments can catalyse change on the ground by creating new incentives – money, recognition or autonomy – that try to persuade public servants to behave in particular ways.

○ *Force:* Where collaboration is necessary but is not happening, governments can force new structures and funding mechanisms on the local level to try and grow a culture of collaboration. In some cases the process is more consensual than the term 'force' would suggest – for instance, children's trusts were centrally imposed but with a high degree of flexibility around implementation.
○ *Augment:* Governments can collaborate with service deliverers and the voluntary sector to augment, complement and supplement existing programmes to deliver policy goals.
○ *Focus:* Governments can focus their delivery systems on a relatively small number of particular goals through concerted periods of political prioritisation, policy development and implementation.

Two of these options – incentivise and force – are already a well-established part of the Whitehall repertoire, relying as they do on inspection, financial incentive and structural reform. They play a vital part in any programme of public service reform, but in isolation they can suffer from serious drawbacks.

Setting too many tightly defined targets or creating too many siloed funding streams leads to fragmentation as different services chase different goals with different funding. National targets can seldom meet all the complexities of local need, and so risk either missing the point or creating unintended consequences. Innovation can be stifled by narrow definitions of high performance.

In any case, the idea that we can somehow force or incentivise effective collaboration is oxymoronic. We can create markets relatively easily, but cooperative behaviour tends to be emergent and organic. It follows from a desire to work together, rather than from new institutions. Those who rely on forcing or incentivising always have to hope that intrinsic motivation will eventually follow from new structures and funding flows – that a revolution of form will somehow result in a revolution of thought and function.

If forcing and catalysing are essentially strategies that seek to make frontline staff conform to central goals, then augmenting and focusing are aimed at guiding delivery systems towards shared goals through discussion and negotiation. If forcing government sees itself as handing down instructions to distant delivery organisations, focusing government sees itself as part of a whole system of delivery, in which the centre is first among equals. Because focusing and augmenting are by their nature collaborative tools, they seem more likely to support frontline collaboration on the ground. Two brief case studies illustrate these principles in action – Finland's experiment with programme management and New Zealand's SKIP programme.

Focusing on Finland[3]

Finland has embarked on what is probably one of the most advanced experiments in project-based government in the developed world – aiming to focus the efforts of its central government departments on delivering a small number of major outcome goals. At the turn of the twenty-first century, the administration of Paavo Lipponen started a major review of the way that Finland's central government worked. It concluded that the country's biggest challenge was its fragmented departmental structure – civil servants did not work together effectively enough, with the result that ministers could not effectively deal with complex problems that fell between department boundaries.

It is a problem that seems to face most governments – the public understands results in terms of the difference government makes to their lives, but government sees the world in terms of departments, targets and indicators. The two do not always connect. Finland's answer was a new way of organising central government business. The endless individual projects and goals were rationalised and supplemented by a small number of key government programmes run from the centre – essentially each new administration would set out three to five major outcome goals it wanted to achieve in its term of office, and would focus effort across government to deliver them.

Lipponen lost the 2004 election and never got the chance to implement his scheme – that was left to his successor, Matti Vanhannen. Since then, the government has adopted four key programmes: employment, entrepreneurship, civil participation and the information society. Each programme is run by the most relevant minister and a strategic ministerial group representing all the relevant parts of government. A dedicated programme manager is appointed in the lead ministry to coordinate the programme and to liaise with civil servants in other ministries, who carry out the work.

For instance, the civil participation programme is led by the Ministry of Justice, which organises elections. Its programme manager, Seppo Niemelä, has an office in the ministry from which he works with a single member of support staff (recently augmented with a handful of website developers). His programme reflects the government's feeling that quality of Finnish democracy has been neglected, and that the system was in need of a 'general check-up'. Niemelä has little formal power, but a remit and a small budget that allows him to work across other government departments to embed his programme. His proudest achievement so far is establishing civic education as an important topic across the Finnish education system, but his programme has also carried out new research, led work on the electoral system, set up several democracy-focused websites and helped develop work on democracy in schools and municipalities.[4]

Overall, the programme management approach seems to be working. An evaluation in 2005 argued that 'the objective of strengthening the political steering of the central government has been reached to a certain extent at least'.[5] The system also seems to have provided a greater definition of the roles of civil servants and ministers, the former dealing with technical matters and the latter in charge of values and vision. The programme management approach has been supported by a series of mid-term policy forums in which ministers consider whether their policies are making a real impact on Finnish society.

Taken together, it adds up to a system of government that is moving away from the traditional focus on structures, finance and administration, and towards a form of politics based much more on outcomes delivered for the citizen. One key factor in enabling Finland to do this has been the government's relaxed approach to being judged on outcomes, even though ministers clearly cannot control all the factors that influence those outcomes.

This cross-departmental focusing of effort provides a formal, political incentive to deliver cross-cutting policy objectives, going beyond joint research and report writing to the beginning of a more networked style of implementation. Speak to programme managers in departments and the prime minister's office and it becomes clear that they believe the system is beginning to drive very real cultural change across the Finnish civil service. Not because of strong central figures – although these are important – but because the system is helping to put outcomes before structures.

Augmenting in New Zealand

Developing more effective central strategy is one thing, but connecting that strategy to large numbers of delivery agencies and local authorities is quite another. Policies that don't bridge the false divide with implementation are doomed to failure. That is why central departments need to learn to collaborate not only with each other, but with councils, hospitals, primary care trusts and other public organisations – working with delivery systems to learn from and augment work that is already happening on the ground.

New Zealand's SKIP programme –Strategies with Kids, Information for Parents – provides a model for augmenting existing work. The programme was aimed at encouraging families to use safe and effective alternatives to physical discipline with their children. It was originally designed by the country's Child, Youth and Family Department as a mass media campaign due to launch in 2003. But early that year, consultations with the wider childcare sector revealed very deep doubts about whether a media campaign would be effective – the consultation recommended a more practical, community-based approach.

The strategy was revised. By the beginning of 2004 the SKIP programme had mutated into a small policy team, housed in the Ministry of Social Development (MSD) and staffed partly by relatively new policy advisers with non-governmental organisation (NGO) experience. The team had good networks with the relevant childcare organisations and a budget inherited from the defunct mass media campaign. What it didn't have was time or a comfortable institutional home – the programme was under extremely high pressure to deliver, and the team was new and somewhat isolated within the MSD.

What happened next was an object lesson in getting quick results through augmenting existing work on the ground – not creating new architectures of delivery, or calling for massive cultural or programme change, but working with existing providers to create what is now widely regarded as a very successful programme. Rather than try and set up a new delivery system, the SKIP team adopted an 'augment, compliment, supplement' intervention model – working with NGOs and other children's service providers, they sought to guide and add value to what was already being done in the field.

The schemes that would deliver SKIP on the ground were co-designed by the policy team and NGOs themselves. Organisations with an interest such as Barnados and Plunket were given resources to examine where they could build SKIP into their existing programmes of work.

Charities got the resources and time to consider their offer, and the fact that the money was coming from government created opportunities for the policy team to work alongside people from the third sector, helping to manage risks and develop stronger relationships.

This wasn't just a free-for-all – providers were guided by a shared brand and a set of practical materials, tools and methods. Everyone involved in the project quickly bought into the slogan: 'SKIP – what children spontaneously do when they are truly happy'. And by ensuring that 'SKIP kits' were provided early in the process, containing pamphlets, videos, papers and guides, the policy team ensured a high degree of buy-in to the basic building blocks of the programme.

The result was a 'tight–loose–tight' framework – the programme goals and tools were relatively fixed, but deliverers had a large degree of freedom about exactly how they implemented the programme. Innovation was explicitly allowed, provided it contributed to the overall goal. SKIP also allowed the government access to a range of channels for contacting and influencing parents that might have taken years to develop through a traditional public sector programme.

The programme design worked because it created space for collaborative design and innovation from the start. This was reinforced by a central government policy team that already had strong NGO experience and a strong culture of team-based working and learning.

An evaluation[6] of the project argues that the SKIP programme's success lay in the ability of central policy-makers to create three positive feedback loops between themselves and the NGOs they were working with:

○   By investing in the capabilities of their NGO partners, the SKIP team created a reflective, collaborative service-planning process that augmented and amplified existing systems, services and practices.

○   By developing the delivery programmes in partnership, the SKIP team helped its partners to feel that they were part of creating a joint programme, in which each player had their unique perspective and skills to bring to the table.

○   By allowing providers to try a variety of ways to get to the same goal, and encouraging learning through workshops and training, SKIP drove up the capacity of the whole system of delivery while building a sense of participation in a social movement.

The result, according to the evaluation, was that the programme delivered a major impact through a relatively small investment of government time and energy.

There are some powerful lessons we might learn from SKIP. The first is that collaborative policy-making and service design can be a potent tool for getting the buy-in of wider delivery systems. It has the potential to powerfully motivate professionals by giving them a sense of ownership and freedom to innovate, while simultaneously ensuring a degree of central control and guidance over the process.

Another lesson is about the power of outsiders. The SKIP policy team did not feel bound by state service conventions. While government departments are notoriously secretive about their policy-making process, SKIP felt able to openly discuss the process with its partners and the outside world as it developed its programme.

Finally, there is a lesson here about harnessing existing relationships and skills, rather than developing them from scratch. The New Zealand government could have wasted a lot of time trying to duplicate the relationships with parents that the NGOs already had – by tapping into charity expertise it saved time and money, delivering a more effective service in the process.

Putting it all together

The point of these case studies is not to propose the wholesale replacement of one set of central government management techniques – force and incentivise – with another – augment and focus. Whitehall will always need access to a wide range of levers of change, and often incentivising or forcing will be the most appropriate.

But as the development of a more localist approach to government continues, based on local solutions to complex problems and a more consensual approach to relationships between the locality and the centre, it seems likely that the value of managing networks through augmentation and focusing techniques will become much clearer. They allow local providers freedom to innovate around key goals, while creating a rolling conversation between local and centre that allows for risk management, disciplining innovation and learning from practice at the front line.

Put these two case studies together and we might have the basis of a new approach to governing – what we might call 'networked policy-making'. Governments that want to be judged on their ability to solve a particularly complex problem – say obesity or anti-social behaviour – might convene a network of ministers and policy-makers from across Whitehall and the wider public sector. Led by the most relevant minister and with a small secretariat, the network would use systems analysis to identify the people throughout the delivery system who are in key positions to drive change. For instance, if the reform programme involves engaging with local government, then the network would probably include a range of local government officials at all relevant levels.

Working together electronically, or through secondments and practical learning, policy networks would be able to focus the energy of the whole delivery system on solving the problem, as well as readily identifying what is already being done and providing easy access to information about what's happening on the ground for Whitehall policy-makers.

Staff in a Whitehall policy network would be involved in rapid, participative programmes of policy development, implementation and learning. Because they would involve key players from across the system, they would not only create policy, but also develop a pool of delivery staff who have a deep understanding of the approach and some degree of commitment to its success. The networks would be time-limited, with their budgets and lifespan related to their success, and the assumption would be that they would wind up once their job was done.

This kind of policy network would model collaboration at the heart of government, and should over time help to create a much deeper culture of networked collaboration across Whitehall, both between departments and with the wider public sector.

Of course, the focus on judging government on outcomes – something the Finns have become comfortable with – also implies a quite different kind of politics. The pledge cards of previous British elections made promises of extra police officers, or offered vague hopes about families and prosperity. But under networked policy-making, the pledges are more likely to be a 20 per cent reduction in crime, 60,000 more jobs or a 30 per cent reduction in child poverty. The implications could be profound, but the potential prize is a form of government that can deliver the kind of result the public understands.

Simon Parker is head of public services research at Demos.

Notes

1   Cabinet Office, *Modernising Government* (Norwich: TSO, 1999), see www.archive.official-documents.co.uk/document/cm43/4310/4310-00.htm (accessed 13 Mar 2007).

2   P Wintour, 'New taskforce to focus on alleviation of social exclusion', *Guardian*, 13 Jun 2006, see www.guardian.co.uk/guardianpolitics/story/ 0,,1796143,00.html (accessed 8 Mar 2007).

3   Case study based on author's own interviews and M Harrinvirta and S Kekkonen, 'Evaluating effectiveness of the horizontal policy programmes of the Finnish government', paper presented to the EPGA Study Group on Productivity and Quality in the Public Sector, Ljubljana, 1–4 Sep 2004; and M Harrinvirta and S Kekkonen, 'Government programme as a subject of performance measurement', paper presented to the EPGA Study Group on Productivity and Quality in the Public Sector, Bern, 31 Aug–3 Sep 2005.

4   Finnish Ministry of Justice website: www.om.fi/Etusivu/Ajankohtaista/ Kansalaisvaikuttamisenpolitiikkaohjelma/Hankkeet?lang=en (accessed 19 Feb 2007).

5   Harrinvirta and Kekkonen, 'Government programme as a subject of performance measurement'.

6   Ministry of Social Development, Te Manatū Whakahiato Ora, *Strategies with Kids – Information for Parents (SKIP) Research Report*, prepared by Gravitas Research and Strategy for Centre for Social Research and Evaluation, Te Pokapū Rangahau Arotaki Hapori (Wellington, NZ: MSD, Feb 2005), see www.msd.govt.nz (accessed 10 Mar 2007).

14. Flesh, steel and Wikipedia

How government can make the most of online collaborative tools

Paul Miller and Molly Webb

In February 1996, John Perry Barlow sat typing away at the World Economic Forum in Davos, Switzerland. At the time, he was a technology journalist, pundit and well known as a former lyricist for the Grateful Dead. He was incensed by the new US Telecommunications Act, which had just been passed to include the first censorship of the internet, and decided he was going to do something about it. 'Governments of the Industrial World,' he typed, 'you weary giants of flesh and steel . . . your legal concepts of property, expression, identity, movement, and context do not apply to us. They are all based on matter and there is no matter here.' He posted what he typed on the internet and it spread fast. His *Declaration of the Independence of Cyberspace* became a rallying call for the dot-com boom – an organising mantra for those with a libertarian, new economy, *Wired* magazine sensibility.[1]

Of course, John Perry Barlow was wrong. The internet hasn't swept away government. Instead, every desk in Whitehall now has a computer on it. Every service provided by government is either available online or dependent on the internet for proper management and delivery. Barlow's black or white 'cyberspace versus government' framing of the situation now needs to be replaced by a new understanding of the way that online tools could help government, and in helping government help the rest of us to live the lives we want to lead.

This piece looks at how the collaborative tools that have emerged in the past five years will become the defining challenges and opportunities for governments over the next decade. At the moment the idea of millions of people collaborating for the public good using technology seems mind-boggling. But in the future it will be much less so, as we begin to understand the patterns and motivations of activity that are taking place in projects such as Wikipedia or the open source operating system Linux. These tools are moving on to a new level of maturity as more and more uses for them become apparent.

The wiki way

Wikipedia is a puzzling thing. It seems contrary to conventional economic thinking that over a million articles (that's just the ones in English) could be created for such a tiny investment, by channelling the creative energy of large numbers of amateurs into such a large, complex project, without traditional hierarchical organisation. It does so by using simple-to-use online collaborative tools. But what can Wikipedia teach government about collaboration?

Wikipedia owes its success to lower barriers to entry for people who want to work together in creating and sharing new knowledge. The technology behind Wikipedia is cheap, simple to use and interactive. It doesn't matter who you are or where you are. Provided who have access to the web (and more and more of us do) you can get involved.

Of course, there have been controversies. Jaron Lanier's essay 'Digital Maoism' railed against the idea of digital collectivism.[2] Lanier used the example of his own entry on Wikipedia which insisted he was a film director (he isn't). Lanier kept on changing the entry but somebody else kept on changing it back. Lanier says that this constitutes a fault with Wikipedia but, as others have argued in response to Lanier's piece, anybody coming to the page could have clicked on the 'history' or 'discussion' buttons to see that something unusual was going on. Wikipedia is usually referred to as an online encyclopaedia, but there are problems with that comparison. Wikipedia is in fact a massive conversation about human knowledge and it takes more than a cursory glance at the article page to find out what's going on.

But focusing on the individual possibilities and pitfalls of individual technologies takes us only so far. We need to look at what Robert Wright calls the 'metatechnologies' that will emerge with collaborative tools to allow us to generate and handle greater degrees of social complexity.[3] As he writes: 'Most social institutions have evolved over time to manage one or more social dilemmas in order to maximize benefits for all.' Wikipedia has also evolved a set of social rules, even in its brief history. The most important is the idea of neutral point of view (NPOV), which is the basic criteria for whether something stays on the site or is deleted.

But why does Wikipedia work? What is it that drives people to volunteer their time and knowledge? The value of what Yale law professor Yochai Benkler calls 'social production' has not yet been fully understood, but we do know that when the right feedback is in place, people will participate in the public sphere on their own terms. As Benkler writes: 'What characterises the networked economy is that decentralized individual action – specifically new and important cooperative and coordinate action carried out through radically distributed, nonmarket mechanisms that do not depend on proprietary strategies – plays a much greater role than it did, or could have, in the industrial information economy.'[4]

Wikipedia is just the highest profile example of collaborative technology creating value for its users. Government has also had a few attempts at using collaborative tools – with mixed results.

Don't feed the troll

In August 2006, The UK Department for the Environment, Food and Rural Affairs (Defra) had a go at using a wiki in what will now become the iconic example that every politician and civil servant will point to as a reason for not using wikis for policy-making. After a couple of weeks of being online, the wiki attracted the attention of the libertarian blogger Guido Fawkes, and his audience soon set about defacing the wiki. Guido followed up the episode with a series of posts on blogs and a discussion list about the internet and democracy:

> *The Wiki idea is a good one for collaborative projects. Politics is not collaborative. The reality is that politics is a clash of ideas and ideology as well as parties. Only a deluded wonk would overlook that non-trivial detail. Wikis can only effectively work as policy development tools when used by a community with common values. The policy-making political class do not have common values. So if you invite those who oppose your ideas to contribute to refining them you should not be surprised when they seek to frustrate your objectives.[5]*

He has obviously put some thought into this position, but Guido overlooks the fact that politics is only intermittently as red in tooth and claw as he supposes. His brand of politics is confrontational, but most peoples' isn't. Democracy is about achieving the things you can't achieve alone – security, education, healthcare, building infrastructure and in order to do those things you need to collaborate with other people. Government is the way we do that. Politics isn't a clash of ideas and ideology – it's a way of mediating between differences without resorting to violence.

What the Defra wiki episode proves is that collaboration requires trust and reciprocity. Online tools remove technological barriers, but not the old social ones, including the disconnect between people and politics. We have to contend with that now as much as ever. Some people won't treat exercises to open up policy-making to a wider community in the spirit it is intended and – as Guido's effort shows – they will attempt to disrupt them. An old rule of thumb in the early days of online message boards was that every internet discussion will end up with someone likening someone else to Hitler. Certainly, a quick scan through the toxic comments on the *Guardian*'s foray into blogging through their Comment is Free site[6] is enough to make any public sector official weighing up the risks of online media wince and put away their chequebook.

In conventional messaging terms, collaborative technologies put government on the back foot, because they give an instant opportunity to respond. It used to be that news was funnelled through a few broadcasters and a handful of newspapers. As Alastair Campbell and his generation showed there was at least some possibility of controlling the messages being communicated through that group.

But today, government – like any other institution – has to contend with millions of pro-am commentators and journalists turning stones they never even knew were there. Even Guido has come in for some so-called 'astro-turfing' when institutional commenters pretend to be ordinary 'grass-roots' members of the public when in fact they're supporting a preordained line to try and discredit or support particular pieces of information or opinions.

The Defra wiki was locked after the initial vandalism to prevent more damage and the most offensive material (including a swastika graphic) removed. It is now open again and seems to be providing a useful forum for the purpose it was intended – to discuss and develop the idea of an environmental contract between government and citizens.[7]

The end of consultation

The New Labour administration has been characterised by an infatuation with consultation. The aim of this – to open up decisions to citizens – has been admirable, but the execution often lousy. Consultation has become an add-on at the end of decision-making rather than the starting point and a consistent process throughout policy-making. It is still all too common for consultations to take place in drafty community centres with a table at the front and lines of plastic chairs for the consultees. They are still set up con-frontationally with a suspicion on the part of participants that they are being brought in to tick a 'consultation' box on an already done deal.

The reason for the failures of consultation can be explained in part because of what James Boyle describes as an 'openness aversion'. He writes: 'We are likely to undervalue the importance, viability and productive power of open systems, open networks and non-proprietary production.'[8] He asks readers to go back and imagine themselves as a decision-maker in 1991:

> *You have to design a global computer network. One group of scientists describes a system that is fundamentally open – open protocols and systems so anyone could connect to it and offer information or products to the world. Another group – scholars, businessmen, bureaucrats – points out the problems. Anyone could connect to it. They could do anything. There would be porn, piracy, viruses and spam. Terrorists could put up videos glorifying themselves. Your activist neighbour could compete with* The New York Times *in documenting the Iraq war. Better to have a well-managed system, in which official approval is required to put up a site; where only a few actions are permitted; where most of us are merely recipients of information; where spam, viruses, piracy (and innovation and anonymous speech) are impossible. Which would you have picked?*[9]

Very few of us given the choice would have picked the world wide web. It seems counterintuitive to allow non-experts to run amok, communicating and collaborating without filtering or mediation. Yet think of all the positive impact the web has had, both economically and socially. Likewise, there is plenty of promise for greater use of collaborative tools by government. Perhaps the most useful thing will be to change the culture of the civil service and public sector institutions away from consultation towards participation.

However, the pressure for this change of culture and the tools to help achieve it, at least so far, seem to come mainly from outside large government institutions. Guido Fawkes and other political bloggers are great examples of using online tools to encourage a community to delve beneath the surface of government's broadcast model tools of communication to find out what is going on. The charity MySociety[10] has developed a whole range of tools that give citizens new ways of interacting with public bodies from Parliament through to local councils. One of the most high profile of these is TheyWorkForYou,[11] which simply uses information already provided by government and makes it more usable and interactive – allowing the public easier access to basic data they can use to hold their representatives to account. But this is just the first stage.

'Web 2.0' is the business buzzword for online products and services that exploit more fully than ever before the properties of networks. The internet has always been used for collaboration, in fact it was founded for that purpose. But we are starting to more effectively exploit some of the properties of this decentralised network. Tim O'Reilly describes these as the core competencies of 'web 2.0' companies; the most interesting for our purposes are:

O   having control over unique, hard-to-recreate data sources
     that get richer as more people use them
O   trusting users as co-developers
O   harnessing collective intelligence
O   leveraging the long tail through customer self-service.[12]

What this means for 'users' (or citizens) is that we see the value of our participation. Each of our actions contributes to an overall better service. The more information Google's search engine has about the linking habits of website users, the more useful it becomes. The more people's buying habits are monitored on Amazon, the better the recommendations to other buyers.

We can expect more and more Web 2.0, collaborative applications with relevance to government and public services to emerge.

Demos and collaborative tools

For over a decade Demos has been a pamphlet machine. Now we're trying to do things differently. Many of the changes we've made to the way we do things have been no brainers. Putting the pamphlets online was the first step, setting up a blog to give people the chance to comment on ideas before they were published was another. Both were cheap to do but increased the reach of our work massively and on more than one occasion led to valuable additions to our ideas that, had we kept the process hidden inside the organisation, wouldn't have happened. We decided to take this further by integrating blogs into each project. Where we used to reach out to our audience with an email update, we have added new routes – RSS subscriptions for projects, press releases as well as the blog, and audio podcasts. Social tagging, allowing us to generate new themes each time we expand areas of work, gives the audience more opportunities to find what they are looking for.

Opening our website therefore had two main outcomes. First, it became a valuable research tool, which meant that we were talking to more people during the course of research, making our final project outputs better. Our creative commons licence and blogging revealed the networks around us, so people could circulate ideas relevant to their particular interests. This in turn opens new avenues for comment and criticism. Second, we could see an increasingly useful role linking conversations between disciplines and across sectors. We will continue to build on this, allowing our networks to link to one another.

People making policy

All this means that policy-making will look very different in ten years' time. Even though technologies such as wikis, blogs, RSS and the like are nothing new, we are just at the beginning of the collaborative, participative internet. The internet and the possibilities it enables are changing because they have opened up the possibility of easy collaboration to many millions more people.

As more and more people encounter collaborative tools in their everyday lives – to download music, share video files, buy and sell shares, donate money to charity and organise events online – our expectations for connection and engagement are shifting. In the context of the networked and decentralised vision, collaborative technology will have an instrumental role in:

o   closing the last mile of social engagement – lowering the barriers to entry for conversation, volunteering and learning
o   diversifying and broadening legitimacy and accountability – holding elected representatives and appointees to account in new ways
o   creating new sources of demand, which when linked together in the right way, create new opportunities of supply – government must be on the lookout for the new demands outside of voting, and how they can respond.

Government will also have to adapt to changes in style of communication. Blogging language is also infiltrating newspapers and broadcast media as programmes and columns are published online in blog format as well as in less interactive form. This clash can be just as explosive as the one between ministers and political bloggers. Press releases jar against the prevailing wisdom of the web for straightforward communication. When something reads as being self-promotional or uncritical, it will attract attacks and criticism. Mixing civil service communication style and the internet is like going to the pub with friends and one person around the table insisting on speaking in Iambic pentameters. It's just a bit weird.

But rather than simply a flowering of bottom-up activity, the real implications of social media for government and other large organisations is that they provide a way of navigating the point where top down meets bottom up. If government treats the public as both consumers and producers of services, we tap into 'I will if you will' awareness, or 'will–will' solutions. Government and individuals are partners. Online collaboration and networking tools provide us with a vision for society that runs counter to a paternal or electoral model. They point to a participative future.

Paul Miller is a Demos Associate. Molly Webb is a Demos researcher.

Notes

1   For the full story see F Turner, *From Counterculture to Cyberculture: Stewart Brand, the Whole Earth Network, and the rise of digital utopianism* (Chicago: Chicago University Press, 2006).

2   J Lanier, 'Digital Maoism: the hazards of the new online collectivism', *Edge: the third culture*, 30 May 2006, available at www.edge.org/3rd_culture/lanier06/lanier06_index.html (accessed 11 Mar 2007).

3   R Wright, *Nonzero: The logic of human destiny* (New York: Pantheon, 1999).

4   Y Benkler, *The Wealth of Networks* (Yale: Yale University Press, 2006).

5   Quoted at http://simondickson.wordpress.com/2006/09/02/guidos-gang-mob-censorship/feed/ (accessed 13 Mar 2007).

6   See www.guardian.co.uk/commentisfree (accessed 13 Mar 2007).

7   See http://wiki.defra.gov.uk/WikiHome (accessed 13 Mar 2007).

8   J Boyle, 'A closed mind about an open world', *Financial Times*, 7 Aug 2006.

9   Ibid.

10 See www.mysociety.org/ (accessed 13 Mar 2007).

11 See www.theyworkforyou.com/ (accessed 13 Mar 2007).

12 See www.oreillynet.com/pub/a/oreilly/tim/news/2005/09/30/what-is-web-20.html (accessed 11 Mar 2007).

15. The co-production paradox

Sophia Parker

A village policeman decided that he wanted to find out more about the concerns of local residents, in order to understand how he could be most helpful. Through a series of conversations he discovered that their biggest worry, by some distance, was speeding in the village. He agreed that he would set himself up in a siding with a speed gun and catch the offending motorists, in a quest to reduce the problem. However, after a week of doing this, it emerged that in fact most of the people he had booked were themselves residents of the village.

From local government reforms to the comprehensive spending review, from public service reform to community cohesion, the rhetoric of user empowerment and citizen engagement is a major part of this government's agenda. But as this brief story demonstrates, collaboration between the state and citizens is rarely a straightforward affair. People say one thing and do another; their wishes for themselves do not always align with their wishes for the community in which they live. At a point where the public policy world is at risk of treating collaboration between state and citizens as a panacea, the complexity of who we are and what we think must not be forgotten. Enhancing opportunities for the state to work together with citizens may facilitate a fresh view of what the issues are, but this view is no less complex than the more traditional ways of seeing the business of government. Indeed it demands new skills for the state and citizens alike, and the ability to recognise and value new forms of evidence and insight at a much earlier stage in the processes of decision-making and policy development.

As many of the other essays in this book show, collaboration between the state and citizens is not easy. Working together takes time, effort and know-how – qualities that most of us feel we have in short supply. But despite the effort that collaboration takes, it is a critical part of renewing the legitimacy and purpose of government in an era of declining trust and interaction between the state and citizens. It is only through such collaboration that that path is opened up for improved services which are both more efficient and more personal. However collaboration is about more than a reform agenda alone: it has a moral dimension that is about empowering people to shape their own lives and participate in the creation of the public realm. If standardisation and mass production were the defining characteristics of our relationship to the state in the twentieth century, we need to make collaboration and participation the leitmotifs of the twenty-first century.

An uncertain relationship

While collaboration in theory may be an attractive agenda for government, the health of the relationship between the state and citizens should give some cause for concern. Too often it appears to be characterised by frustration, anger and simple confusion. Too often it feels far from collaborative, with people branding the state as 'distant' or 'uncaring', and the state struggling to understand or recognise how the consequences of particular policies and initiatives play out in the everyday lives of each of us.

The story of the inconsistent villagers is reflected in patterns and shifting attitudes to collaboration and participation. When asked about desire to participate, citizens complain of power resting elsewhere, of too few opportunities to get involved and shape decisions. A mere one in five of us feel satisfied with the opportunities to participate in local decision-making.[1] In a recent poll, 80 per cent of respondents supported the notion of elected councillors setting local priorities, and 73 per cent of people supported the idea of neighbourhoods having more control over the provision and budgets of services.[2] Similarly, as individuals accessing services we want more say: 91 per cent of people with long-term health conditions would like more involvement in decisions about their treatment, for example.[3]

Despite this stated desire for more involvement, people's activities tell a different story. We are voting less than ever before, and this is a relatively recent phenomenon. Between the 1980s and 2001 turnout tumbled from 80 per cent to 61 per cent;[4] 49 per cent of people do not believe that their local council does enough for people 'like me', and levels of satisfaction and trust continue to fall.[5]

This perception that power rests elsewhere is emerging at precisely the time that collaboration between the state and citizens is ever more urgent. Governing in the twenty-first century is no mean feat. Increasingly the kinds of challenges society faces cut across institutional and indeed state boundaries. And increasingly the kinds of problems governments are expected to solve require people's participation as well. For example:

○ *Health:* The current UK system of healthcare was developed in an era where the predominant concern was acute illness. In the twenty-first century, the overwhelming concern is chronic illness and 'lifestyle diseases' – issues the current system is ill-equipped to deal with. For example, diabetes accounts for 9 per cent of the NHS's budget today, but on projected figures that is set to increase to 25 per cent by 2020. Overall, by 2025, at the current rate of change, healthcare will represent 12–15 per cent of our GDP.

○ *Care:* An ageing population, combined with a pensions crisis and increasing numbers of women and men working full time, risks creating unsustainable demand on the formal care sector in coming years. Eldercare and childcare are set to represent 5–8 per cent of our GDP by 2025.[6]

In both of these examples, and indeed many of the other most pressing issues – energy supply, climate change and community cohesion – it is clear that outcomes simply cannot be achieved through applying greater pressure to existing models of public services, or trying to squeeze yet more productivity out of them: improvement alone isn't enough. As Derek Wanless argued in his 2002 review of the health service: 'The key differentiator for success over the next 20 years is not how the health service responds, but how the public and patients do.'[7] We need radically new models of service.

These new models will emerge only from the state working more closely with citizens, investing time and resources into developing the capacity for collaboration and finding new ways of tapping into the energies and motivations of people, encouraging them to participate in the common enterprise of positive outcomes. As Sue Goss has argued:

> *Many of the new priorities – 'respect', an end to 'binge drinking', recycling, improved public health – cannot be achieved by a smart government delivery machine; they require changes in behaviour from the public. This means not simply reconsidering how to deliver using public or even private resources, but how to access the 'free' resources of public energy, engagement and action.*[8]

So if people want to get more involved, and if the state needs people to collaborate more in order to achieve outcomes, why is it that the full potential of state–citizen collaboration has yet to be realised? The answer to this rests with the timid and partial way government has embraced the co-production agenda. People are quick to recognise an empty promise of greater power, where consultation bears no reflection on final decisions, and where bottom-up deliberation continues to be trumped by top-down directives. Collaboration continues to be viewed by government as an additional task to do, rather than the central way in which their business is done. And this in turn creates a gap between the promise and reality of greater collaboration. It is into this gap that the vital resources of trust, energy and satisfaction fall.

Approaches so far

At different times, this government has relied on various models of change to bring about improvements in public services and the public realm more generally. In the early years there was a strong emphasis on a 'top-down' model of change. The route to equality of opportunity and better outcomes was through a series of discrete interventions to make the existing system of public services work better and more equally. The language of reform was mechanistic – with talk of 'levers', 'machinery of government' and 'delivery' – and the approach did little to alter the dominant dynamic between state and citizen, where 'the gentleman in Whitehall knew best' and there was little talk of citizens having a greater say in the design of public services; where 'devolution' was about Scotland and Wales, rather than neighbourhoods and 'very local' government.

We have come a long way from the overly simplistic and top-down models of reform that characterised the early years of New Labour. As time has gone on this government has sought to introduce further pressures for reform: 'bottom-up' pressure in the form of enhanced mechanisms for 'choice and voice'; and lateral pressure through the emphasis on contestability and diversification of providers. Strategies for improvement across government departments now seek to deploy all three approaches to bring about positive social change.

Despite the journey towards increasing citizen involvement in the design and delivery of public services, it is still the case that the full potential of state–citizen collaboration has not been realised. There are three principal, and related, limitations that are currently holding back the transformative potential of genuine, deep collaboration between citizens and the state.

First, there is a lack of investment in capacity-building to enable people to exercise their right to choice and voice. Participating, collaborating, even making decisions as an individual, requires time, confidence and knowledge and these resources are not evenly distributed throughout the population.

Second, the current conception of 'citizen' is too narrow. Too often, government rhetoric sees them as individual consumers; in reality they are both producers and consumers. Someone participating in a smoking cessation course is both consuming a health service and producing a more healthy population. Furthermore not enough is said about the fact that citizens can and should act collectively as well as individually. For example, while it is possible to make decisions and influence services we use as individuals (eg healthcare, schooling), other issues require citizens to exercise voice and choice collectively (eg policing, transport).

Third, there is a risk that the agenda of co-production treats citizen–state collaboration as a managerial tool, or a route to greater efficiency. In fact, as the remainder of this essay indicates, it must be seen as a vital source of public value – far from being a means to a predefined end, collaboration between the state and citizens is the only way to invest in and renew the public realm.

The future

Co-production – the jargon for greater collaboration between the state and its citizens – is not simply an agenda for improvement. It is not about government doing less and pushing greater responsibility onto citizens; rather, it is a vision for transformation, a recasting of the relationship between individuals and the world in which they live. At its best, deep collaboration between citizens and the state is about giving people a chance to play an active role in shaping their own lives. It is about enhancing what Robert Sampson has called collective efficacy – in other words, helping people to make connections between the decisions they make, and the quality of the public realm as it is experienced by others around them.

On that basis, the question is less about how much or how little government should do, and more about what it does. There are two key areas where collaboration between state and citizens could be enhanced to shape a new contract between them: first, public services, and second, civil society more generally. Across both these areas there are four priorities for any government looking to close the chasm that is emerging between citizens and the state.

Enhance opportunities for direct collaboration

There have already been a number of success stories about how people might be empowered to play an active role in the delivery of public services such as healthcare and housing. For example, in the pilot areas for the transfer of housing stock to tenant-led tenant management organisations, 77 per cent of residents believe that the shift has had a positive impact on their quality of life.[9]

Transferring assets to communities is not the only avenue for direct collaboration between citizens and the state. Initiatives such as the Expert Patients programme demonstrate how government can find ways of encouraging citizens to support and enhance particular services. There are many other potential applications of this approach. For example, parents consistently report that they prefer to be supported by other parents than by parenting professionals. Investing in parent-led networks such as Gingerbread or Netmums could be a powerful means of enhancing opportunities for direct collaboration between state and citizens in the creation of positive outcomes.[10]

Beyond public services specifically, there has also been a range of experiments in creating more avenues for citizen collaboration in their local areas – for example, through neighbourhood committees, community representation on local strategic partnerships or foundation hospital boards. More needs to be done to encourage local councils to develop further experiments in mechanisms for citizen involvement to push the aspirations of the local government white paper[11] further, for example around the right to request a review.

Build capacity for more collaboration

The risk is that the capacity for collaboration with the state is unevenly distributed throughout the population. Other Demos research has uncovered a 'rich get richer' effect in participation: once someone has joined one board, they are likely to take on further positions and activities.[12] Therefore there needs to be a sustained investment in capacity-building activities, in order to maximise the benefits of collaboration.

The role of voluntary, community and user-led organisations in this work is central. As John Craig and Paul Skidmore have argued, a key characteristic of this sector is that they 'start with people'.[13] They play a crucial role as 'civic intermediaries' and so can be vital in creating confident, articulate citizens, as well as advocating on their behalf.

The creation of an Office of the Third Sector is a promising sign that government is taking voluntary and community organisations seriously. What it must not forget is that the value of these organisations does not simply rest in being an alternative service delivery arm; they also play a vital role in developing civic capacity. Enhanced citizen collaboration needs a vibrant third sector.

Create more channels for indirect collaboration

An agenda for deeper collaboration between citizens and the state cannot focus only on opportunities for direct involvement. It needs to go wider than this and find new ways of connecting people's insights and feedback about public service experiences to priorities for reform, and embedding these connections into how decisions are made.

The small but emerging discipline of service design offers some powerful reflections on how users can be connected to reform. Service designers spend inordinate amounts of time learning to see services as users do – mapping out user journeys, exploring the emotional aspects of a service experience, gathering data on the interaction between services and people's lives – in order to understand what the real issues are.

By focusing so much on the interactions between services and people's lives, rather than simply the internal workings of that service, it is possible to strengthen the connections across implementation, delivery and policy design.[14] Engagement at the point of delivery is just as important as the more deliberative forms of state–citizen collaboration outlined above.

Therefore more needs to be done to incentivise policy-makers at the local and national level to 'design in' the generation of citizen insights and qualitative data alongside the quantitative performance information that is already gathered. This has significant implications for the skills and capacities of civil servants and local government officials. It also demands that government learns to think in terms of issues rather than silos, and in terms of people rather than process.

Collaborate to innovate

Citizen–state collaboration can support and improve existing models of service and participation in civic society, but the relationship needs to be about more than improvement alone. There is a need for radical innovation as well, in order to generate models of service that will be effective, and deliver significantly better outcomes for less money, in the future.

It used to be the case that innovation was seen as an activity carried out by lone inventors, working for years on a single project and waiting for their 'eureka' moment. However, as the innovation literature has grown, it has become clear that far from innovation being an isolated activity, it is in fact a far more collaborative and iterative process that requires the input of a range of perspectives on any given issue to generate new ideas and practice.

Investment in innovation in the UK is overly focused on product and scientific innovation,[15] despite the fact that the service economy makes up 72 per cent of our GDP, and despite the fact that more than ever there is a need for radical new models of service based on prevention not cure. As the Young Foundation has argued, we urgently need to right the balance and invest more in social innovation in order to meet the challenges we now face.[16]

Involving citizens in the innovation process can yield real results as it brings a new kind of knowledge to the table: it ensures that innovations are grounded in the practical realities of everyday life.

Citizen–state collaboration: an agenda for emotionally intelligent government

Letting citizens into the processes of government and governance implies a new contract between state and citizens, a new relationship that is characterised by greater equality, mutuality and respect.

The points above suggest a practical agenda that this government could focus on to enhance the opportunities for collaboration between state and citizens. However to be successful in developing this agenda there remain two potential stumbling blocks that stem from a long legacy of a paternalistic state and an overly passive conception of citizenship.

First, working with regulators and inspection bodies, government needs to do more to create a single view of progress and problems in the system. At the moment, too often there is a gap between people's experiences of public services and the story told by system measures. As one local authority official put it: 'You might get the three-star CPA [comprehensive performance assessment] ratings but the residents may not think the service is three-star.'[17] It is into this gap that the crucial resource of trust falls. As Peter Taylor-Gooby has argued, such a gap undermines the potential for collaboration as there is a sense that there is one reality for us as citizens, and another for the policy-makers and politicians.[18] Drawing on the huge advances in technology, more work is needed to create 'real time information' to provide transparency to citizens, quality and timely information for professionals and policy-makers, but most importantly, a unified and shared understanding of the key issues.

Second, and related, is the need to broaden our conception of what knowledge matters. An important part of the mass production model that has underpinned UK public services for so long is the separation of production and consumption, and the creation of specialist managers whose identity was defined by access to 'expert' knowledge.

In contrast, the notion of co-production emphasises the fact that production and consumption are inextricably linked. Collaboration between state and citizens will be little more than tokenism unless situated, social knowledge is recognised as being as valuable as analytical and evidence based data.[19]

Overcoming these stumbling blocks opens the door to a renewed politics – one based less on the 'rational man' model that has dominated discussions in recent years, and more based on the values and aspirations of citizens. As the story at the start of this essay illustrated, human nature is rarely logical, and on that basis seeking to create political institutions that are based on rational, detached analysis of the issues is unlikely to engage people or inspire them to participate. As Robin Cook once said: 'A good society isn't defined by its pass rate on performance indicators, but by the values that shape it.'[20]

Forging deeper and stronger collaboration is not just about adding the new resources of people's energies and motivation to the mix, important though this is. There is a moral and political case to be made for state–citizen collaboration: it is about the renewal of our public realm. Through greater participation, people can open up the possibility of playing a more active role in shaping their own lives, and of creating and sharing in the fruits of a more vibrant, interconnected and empathetic civil society.

Sophia Parker is a Demos associate.

Notes

1   H Mulholland, 'Kelly sets out plan to reconnect public with councils', *SocietyGuardian.co.uk*, 23 Oct 2006, available at: http://society.guardian.co.uk/localgovt/story/0,,1929647,00.html (accessed 11 Mar 2007).

2   E Cox, *Empowering Neighbourhoods: Going beyond the double devolution deal* (London: Local Government Information Unit, May 2006), available at www.lgiu.gov.uk/admin/images/uploaded/Empowering%20Neighbourhoods.pdf (accessed 13 Mar 2007).

3   Of 23,000 people with a long-term health condition. Quoted at a Nuffield Trust seminar, 13 Feb 2006.

4   SB Greenberg, CEO Greenberg Quinlan Rosner Research, The Urban Forum Lecture: 'Engaging with disengagement: politics fit for the 21st century', London, 13 Sep 2006.

5   Mulholland, 'Kelly sets out plan to reconnect public with councils'.

6   The figures on GDP come from Geoff Mulgan, director of the Young Foundation.

7   D Wanless, *Securing Our Future Health: Taking a long-term view* (London: HM Treasury, 2002), available at available at www.hm-treasury.gov.uk/consultations_and_legislation/wanless/consult_wanless_final.cfm (accessed 14 Mar 2007).

8   S Goss, 'The reform of public service reform', *Renewal* 12, no 2/3 (2005).

9   Prime Minister's Strategy Unit, *Personal Responsibility and Changing Behaviour: The state of knowledge and its implications for public policy* (London: Cabinet Office, 2004).

10   This was a recommendation in Hannah Green and Sophia Parker, *The Other Glass Ceiling: The domestic politics of parenting* (London: Demos, 2006).

11   Communities and local government, *Strong and Prosperous Communities: The local government white paper* (Norwich: TSO, 2006), available at www.communities.gov.uk/index.asp?id=1503999 (accessed 12 Mar 2007).

12   P Skidmore, K Bound and H Lownsbrough, *Community Participation: Who benefits?* (London: JRF/Demos, 2006).

13   P Skidmore and J Craig, *Start with People: How community organisations put citizens in the driving seat* (London: Demos, 2005).

14   S Parker and J Heapy, *The Journey to the Interface: How public service design can connect users to reform* (London: Demos, 2006).

15   National Endowment for Science, Technology and the Arts, *The Innovation Gap* (London: NESTA, Oct 2006), available at www.nesta.org.uk/informing/policy_and_research/highlights/innovation_gap_report.aspx (accessed 13 Mar 2007).

16   G Mulgan et al, *Social Silicon Valleys* (London: Young Foundation, 2006).

17   Parker and Heapy, *Journey to the Interface*.

18   P Taylor-Gooby, 'The efficiency/trust dilemma', *Health, Risk and Society* 8, no 2 (2006).

19   For more discussion of this point see H Wainwright, *Reclaim the State* (London: Verso, 2003).

20   D Alexander and S Creasy, *Serving a Cause, Serving a Community* (London: Demos, 2006).

16. Evolving the future

Tom Bentley

Late in 2006, the Australian federal government published an advertisement in the *Australian*, the country's national newspaper. It announced a new agreement on social security between the Kingdom of Norway and the Government of Australia, beginning on new year's day 2007. The agreement begins: 'Wishing to strengthen the existing friendly relations between the two countries, and resolved to coordinate their social security systems and to eliminate double coverage for workers, the parties have agreed . . .'

If I meet pension requirements in Norway, I can still receive the benefit if I then move to Australia. If I have worked in both countries, I can add together the years and put them towards entitlements in whichever country I retire in. While the systems remain separate, it becomes possible to personalise my participation in them.

This kind of activity is growing. It illustrates how greater interconnectedness across the world prompts collaboration between governments – separate sovereign entities – in order to solve shared problems and make life easier and better for citizens. Social insurance and welfare, for so long conceived as the product of different nation state systems, are becoming internationalised. The governments do not merge their schemes, or try to run them in exactly the same way. But they agree that time spent working and paying taxes in one country can be treated as equivalent to doing the same in another.

As bilateral agreements between specific governments add up, they slowly contribute to the formation of an institutional environment – a space shaped by rules – which can be far bigger and more significant than any one of its formal elements.

These are collaborative relationships *between* governments, but the same principle applies to collaboration within societies, and within governments themselves; the state is not a single, monolithic entity, but a proliferation of organisations, teams, interests and centres of power. Collaboration between government and society, and between states seeking peace, wealth and security, is as old as states themselves. It is part of the process through which governments have emerged,[1] but it is becoming more important for three linked reasons.

The first is the growth of connectedness, or connexity.[2] If every problem is connected to something or someone else, then collaboration to solve it is logically necessary. Second, networks, especially the internet, make collaboration easier, cheaper and therefore more diverse and wide-ranging through a range of tools, practices and cultures.

Third, reform of the state over the last 30 years has, as Sue Goss points out, pluralised and multiplied the number of agencies involved in public service provision. Privatisation, contestability and decentralisation mean that, where government is seeking to create a public good, it is increasingly likely to do it through collaboration with organisations in other sectors. Changing citizen expectations – of less deference, more flexibility and better service – reinforce this shift.[3]

Vertical and lateral

We as citizens have become used to an image of government which is separate from the rest of society, defined by its coercive nature and its martial roots, logically distinct from the worlds of market and civil society. There are good reasons why governments should be perceived as such, and why they should want to be – to achieve the impartial administration of justice, for example, and to maintain the monopoly on the legitimate use of force by avoiding the capture of power by specific interests in society.[4]

In fact, the need to collaborate is designed into government as a result of democracy and constitutionalism. The separation of powers into distinct, independent entities is the ultimate political design principle for collaboration. It seeks to ensure that no one agency or clique can impose its own priorities wholesale. To put boundaries around institutional authority, we need defined functions and vertical powers. To create solutions across complex fields, they need lateral relationships and capabilities.

Combining these effectively leads to successful government. The consequence is that successful politics and policy require persuasion, bargaining, compromise, sharing of benefits and, even if indirectly, learning between different players and territories.

This need to combine specialisation and integration, command and consent, competition and collaboration casts fresh light on the value of federal systems of government, and points to why they have emerged as a way to balance the competing interests and identities of separate communities with the interests and needs that they simultaneously share. As Robert Wright wryly notes:

> In 1500 BC, there were around 600,000 autonomous polities on the planet. Today, after many mergers and acquisitions, there are 193 autonomous polities. At this rate, the planet should have a single government any day now.[5]

But while the force of history encourages unification, the merger process has been accompanied by enormous growth in the lateral connections and relationships used to manage across and between governments, giving them adaptive flexibility alongside economies of scale. As a result, institutional design has an enormous impact on how a given system solves collective problems. Federal systems such as the US, Swiss, Canadian and Australian, designed pragmatically to give a self-balancing weight to different constituencies, can encourage both competition *and* collaboration between members of the same federation with positive-sum consequences.

Renegotiating the terms of federation, in order to achieve

structural reform which creates positive-sum economic and social effects, provides us with a clear example of the benefits, and the difficulty, of achieving collaborative governance. Australia's current National Reform Agenda, in which federal and state governments of different parties have committed to negotiating shared investment in reforms designed to boost the long-run capabilities of the Australian population through human capital, regulatory and infrastructure investment, provides a working example.[6]

Beyond the current options

All these reasons help to explain why governments have moved significantly towards a fresh emphasis on collaboration in the last decade – an emphasis that is moving from a policy focus on improving 'service' towards the issues of personalisation and co-production that require more radical redesign of services and new organisational forms.

The organisational designs which government can draw on to pursue these relationships are also expanding in range, from contract management and Memoranda of Understanding to joint ventures and a range of network designs. Sir Michael Barber, pioneer of public service reform, recently argued that there are essentially only three models of reform – command and control, quasi-markets and a 'combination of devolution and transparency' – in which governments delegate to or contract with service providers and then hold them accountable.[7]

But there is a much broader range of system models and reform options available if you recognise the range that can evolve, or emerge, from different combinations of Barber's three basic types. If you build an architecture for collaboration, as well as competition and control, and recognise that the strategies of *all* organisations are likely to evolve in response to changing conditions, then a far more diverse range of possibilities comes into view.

This broader view allows us to recognise the range of platforms that government can use to offer services, and the combinations of organisations that can be involved in them. Goldsmith and Eggers, for example, identify channel partnerships, information dissemination networks, supply chains, service contracts and 'civic switchboards' on their spectrum; the burgeoning science of networks could provide many more.[8]

Yet even this range does not cover what is arguably the most important area for the future of public services: the role of government in shaping an environment through which *citizens themselves* can collaborate and produce various kinds of good. This matters because the social and economic conditions that drive collaboration reinforce the need for governments to go beyond their current institutional options.

Citizens innovate through collaboration

These are the conditions that lead Yochai Benkler to advocate social, or 'commons-based' production as the most important new way to meet diverse human needs. The same set of broad changes leads Charles Leadbeater to emphasise the possibilities of mass creativity, or 'We think', in which many institutional and economic barriers to collaborative problem-solving are broken down and collaboration for mutual gain can happen on mass scale and at great distance in everything from the organisation of work and the production of energy to the provision of education.[9]

Benkler argues that this shift allows many more ways for people to meet their own needs by creating services, activities, culture for themselves. He also maintains that these production processes inevitably draw on the resources generated by the creativity of others. These resources are the 'commons' from which we find raw materials to shape our own personal efforts, as well as the comparisons and sources of inspiration which we use to ground our sense of who we are and what we want.

Social production is happening already; in informal networks of learning, social care and work coordination, in sports clubs and local health centres where shared social activities contribute to wellbeing and to better health outcomes. It is intertwined with the architecture of professional service delivery, and often obscured by the collection of statistics which highlight only the more formal processes.

The dominant institutional frameworks through which public responses to human need are pursued – the competitive field of the market and the command-based domain of the state – are too narrow for the reality created by an evolving society. That is why partnership and joint venture have become part of the government repertoire. But crucially, the new forms of production can evolve into larger-scale structures capable of supporting mass-scale activities, and therefore competing with the scale of industrial production or of government procurement, but using quite different rules of participation. As Benkler puts it:

> These architectures and organisational models allow both independent creation that coexists and coheres in usable patterns and interdependent cooperative enterprises in the form of peer-production processes.[10]

Traditionally, the scope for activity driven by 'non-instrumental' motivations is ascribed to the civic realm and third sector of non-profit, non-governmental organisations (and to the private realm of family and friendship networks). But the boundaries of this category are fuzzy, ranging from the tiny to the multinational, and intersecting with state funding and market trading in numerous ways. The emergence of collaborative production means that such 'social production' processes can be intertwined with activities and institutions that are grounded firmly in both market and state, not hived off artificially into a catch-all category of third or community sector organisations.

The significance of this shift for the shape of what we currently call public services is huge, given the stage that public service reform has reached in many countries. The monolithic, catch-all provision of the past is widely recognised as an undesirable platform for the future. But the current range of reform options, particularly those focused solely on the privatisation of services and assets and shifting the burden of risk onto individuals, is equally unpalatable.

Yet in countries which are ageing, diversifying and shifting further towards service-based economies, new ways to intertwine productive economic capacity with social investment are urgently needed. The greatest need is exactly at the interface between self-provision by individuals and families and formal service provision.

This is partly because the pattern of human need is shifting, in wealthy industrialised societies, in ways that make the traditional methods of paying for public services unsustainable, and the traditional methods of organising and regulating them ineffective. As the burden of disease shifts towards the chronic, and the nature of work becomes intertwined with the expectation of continuous learning, new patterns of production for these goods are needed which can simultaneously personalise and replenish the commons on which they draw. This should be the goal of the collaborative state.

A glance at some of the other pieces in this collection, and at Demos's past catalogue, shows that this is exactly what is happening, from below, in the field of public service provision. Collaborative service design by organisations operating together in local areas is the foundation of effective co-production between citizens and government. The collaborative state has to include those organisations and networks that can mediate between individual need and universal rules; it is through that process of mediation that service can be personalised, responsibility shared and value co-created.

But two great historical barriers stand in the way of the ability of governments to practise and promote collaboration across all their functions. The first is that the establishment of modern, reliable, professionally run states rests on the ability to prevent corruption, which is a form of illicit collaboration. This means that many of the protocols, routines and instincts of government are dedicated to screening out unwanted contact, or channelling it through dedicated routes, reinforcing what can be experienced from the outside as rigid and opaque.

Second, government grew through the nineteenth and twentieth centuries around the idea of functionally based, professional services in which expert knowledge was organised into separate units – silos – and governed through vertical chains of hierarchy and accountability.

An unholy alliance of history, accountability and power combine to hold this approach in place. Of course, preserving accountability to parliament and encouraging responsible use of public budgets is important, especially in complex systems. But there is a simpler reason for the stasis, one which public servants and politicians can rarely own up to in public: the struggle for power. One former Conservative cabinet minister remarked to me soon after the 1997 election that trying to reform Whitehall departments meant dealing with 'feudal baronies', a remark that chimes uncomfortably with Henry Tam's observation that the barons have become postmodern under New Labour.

While political power is measured by the size of the departmental portfolio, and civil service careers progress towards the pinnacle of hierarchy through control of ever-expanding chunks of organisation, the tendency towards organisational co-production at the top of government is always going to be limited. This, of course, is well known, but how to overcome it is not. It matters not so much because everything depends on these tiers of government, but because they reinforce a culture and a set of assumptions which weaken the possibilities of collaboration elsewhere.

Officially, government still lives in a Newtonian world where every reaction produces its own absolute effects, which should be separable and measurable in isolation from all other activities. In this world, policy rationally sets the objectives of delivery organisations, allocates resources, management control and accountability, and the outcomes of, say, a hospital reorganisation or a crime reduction target should be achieved through the vertical transfer of instructions and incentives down and up the chain of command.

This tendency is reinforced by the 'principal–agent' mindset of the New Public Management, in which the strategic task is always to establish who is really in charge, a precondition allocating 'operational' accountability. But as Charles Sabel argues, the separation of strategy from execution is repeatedly undermined by the realities of implementation and the fact that the operators are usually those with the greatest circumstantial knowledge about how things work.[11]

The erosion of these assumptions is part of a much deeper shift in our understanding of the nature of organisations, away from the attempt to make them work like machines following commands, and towards a view of more complex sets of relationships, in which people act for a mix of motivations and where change arises from both conscious, formal decision-making and from a constant process of adaptation, adjustment and improvisation.

Beyond this shift, as Sabel points out, 'the canonical form of this organization is federated and open'. While higher level organisations (parliament, government departments) set general outcome goals and boundaries of action, the ability of the overall system to find effective solutions, and to adapt successfully to changes in the external environment, depends on the ongoing interaction between rule setting from above and lesson learning, in the light of experience, from below.

As Sabel argues:

> These federated organizations respond to the problem of bounded rationality not primarily by decomposing complex tasks into simple ones, but rather by creating search networks that allow actors quickly to find others who can in effect teach them what to do because they are already solving a like problem.[12]

A collaborative state is one that can reshape its own actions, investments and architecture around this search for continuous improvement through learning.

Evolving the future

But can government really embrace such a future? Private firms are arguably far more comfortable in a Darwinian world, not least because survival of the fittest is an accepted principle. Can the art of governing develop into the capacity to design rules and project goals for complex sets of organisations, learning systematically from their efforts and designing regimes for collaboration that maximise the public value they create?

The range of current practice suggests that collaborative innovation is rich, varied and growing. The growing difficulty of maintaining traditional service models will continue to prompt innovation from below. Much harder to achieve, though, is the adaptation of large-scale institutional architecture. But even here the future of collaboration is more likely to evolve from the growth and spread of new practices than from wholesale structural change imposed from above.

The key is to understand how to use policy design and the management of implementation to model, incentivise and then learn systematically from patterns of collaborative action. As these approaches become more visible and more successful, the feedback they create on what succeeds needs to be channelled systematically into the recurrent decision-making cycles such as budget allocation. Unfortunately, the connections between evidence, practice and budget allocation remain weak in most systems.

But opportunities to reshape the state through collaboration abound. There is no reason, for example, why American cities, Australian states and the EU should not collaborate to develop solutions to climate change through carbon trading; it is already beginning to happen. Equally, it should become a core part of government's role to co-design and invest in the architecture, enabling the wider public realm of institutions and organisations to collaborate in ways that make co-production, or social production, a visible feature of everyday life.

Governments can do this by:

o redesigning public procurement processes to encourage federations and network-based consortia to come forward with innovative solutions to cross-cutting public needs
o experimenting with changed departmental structures

based more heavily on teams and projects, which reward
effective cross-organisational collaboration and make
senior managers accountable when it fails

O   adjusting parliamentary accountability regimes to seek
evidence of learning and intelligent explanation, rather
than mechanically searching for proof of the gap between
rule and reality

O   building 'open architecture' designed to make
collaboration easier by helping public agencies, firms,
civic organisations and so on to find each other on the
basis of working on similar problems

O   investing in modelling and forecasting techniques which
examine the behaviour of complex fields of agents
adapting to various conditions and environmental
changes, rather than the limiting assumptions of classical
economic theory or the linear predictions of traditional
implementation planning

O   seeking to design public agencies capable of taking a long-
term, population-based approach to the outcomes they
seek, for example in preventive health care, and rewarding
them with assets and new responsibilities in return for
long-term outcome improvement

O   building 'learning systems' which seek to nurture and
scale up innovation through rapid cycles of design,
application and feedback across groups of organisations
working on a common problem, and rewarding consortia
that come up with successful innovations.

The collaborative state mixes up many roles, powers and assumptions
that have held for more than a century of modern government. But
the forces undermining these modern myths have already been
unleashed. Reformers are already seeking new routes through which
to achieve large-scale change, and new models for collective provision
in diverse societies. These new patterns, driven by both collaboration
and competition, will emerge from below.

Policy, regulation, funding and learning systems then have a huge impact on how they are taken up and spread, and who gets access to the value that they create. Collaboration, pursued with discipline, is the route to the redesign of our large-scale services and governance structures. The challenge of leadership is to focus it on the problems that government exists to solve.

Tom Bentley is an executive director in Victoria's Department of Premier and Cabinet and director of applied learning at ANZSOG, the Australia and New Zealand School of Government. He writes here in a personal capacity.

Notes

1   R Wright, *NonZero: The logic of human destiny* (New York: Vintage, 2001).
2   G Mulgan, *Connexity: How to Live in a Connected World* (Cambridge, MA: Harvard Business School Press, 1997).
3   S Zuboff and J Maxmin, *The Support Economy: Why corporations are failing individuals and the next episode of capitalism* (London: Allen Lane, 2003).
4   Recent events in Thailand and Northern Ireland, one a swift takeover of government by the army, the other a reconstitution of policing to break with a past marred by collusion and systematic bias, show the ongoing relevance of such risks.
5   Wright, *NonZero*.
6   The Victorian government, for which I work part time, is a leading player in these negotiations.
7   M Barber, 'Reform of our public services is a test for managers', *Financial Times*, 27 Sep 2006, available at www.mckinsey.com/locations/ukireland/publications/pdf/FT_RP2363.pdf (accessed 13 Mar 2007).
8   S Goldsmith and D Eggers, *Government by Network: The new public management imperative* (Cambridge, MA: Deloitte/Ash Institute for Democratic Governance and Innovation, Harvard University, 2004), available at www.rppi.org/netgovfinal.pdf (accessed 11 Mar 2007).
9   See www.wethinkthebook.net/home.aspx (accessed 13 Mar 2007).
10   Y Benkler, *The Wealth of Networks* (London: Yale University Press, 2006).
11   C Sabel, 'Beyond principal–agent governance: experimentalist organizations, learning and accountability', WRR discussion paper, 2004, available at www2.law.columbia.edu/sabel/papers/Sabel.definitief.doc (accessed 11 Mar 2007).
12   Ibid.

DEMOS – Licence to Publish

1. **Definitions**
   a   **"Collective Work"** means a work, such as a periodical issue, anthology or encyclopedia, in which the Work in its entirety in unmodified form, along with a number of other contributions, constituting separate and independent works in themselves, are assembled into a collective whole. A work that constitutes a Collective Work will not be considered a Derivative Work (as defined below) for the purposes of this Licence.
   b   **"Derivative Work"** means a work based upon the Work or upon the Work and other pre-existing works, such as a musical arrangement, dramatization, fictionalization, motion picture version, sound recording, art reproduction, abridgment, condensation, or any other form in which the Work may be recast, transformed, or adapted, except that a work that constitutes a Collective Work or a translation from English into another language will not be considered a Derivative Work for the purpose of this Licence.
   c   **"Licensor"** means the individual or entity that offers the Work under the terms of this Licence.
   d   **"Original Author"** means the individual or entity who created the Work.
   e   **"Work"** means the copyrightable work of authorship offered under the terms of this Licence.
   f   **"You"** means an individual or entity exercising rights under this Licence who has not previously violated the terms of this Licence with respect to the Work, or who has received express permission from DEMOS to exercise rights under this Licence despite a previous violation.
2. **Fair Use Rights.** Nothing in this licence is intended to reduce, limit, or restrict any rights arising from fair use, first sale or other limitations on the exclusive rights of the copyright owner under copyright law or other applicable laws.
3. **Licence Grant.** Subject to the terms and conditions of this Licence, Licensor hereby grants You a worldwide, royalty-free, non-exclusive, perpetual (for the duration of the applicable copyright) licence to exercise the rights in the Work as stated below:
   a   to reproduce the Work, to incorporate the Work into one or more Collective Works, and to reproduce the Work as incorporated in the Collective Works;
   b   to distribute copies or phonorecords of, display publicly, perform publicly, and perform publicly by means of a digital audio transmission the Work including as incorporated in Collective Works;
   The above rights may be exercised in all media and formats whether now known or hereafter devised. The above rights include the right to make such modifications as are technically necessary to exercise the rights in other media and formats. All rights not expressly granted by Licensor are hereby reserved.
4. **Restrictions.** The licence granted in Section 3 above is expressly made subject to and limited by the following restrictions:
   a   You may distribute, publicly display, publicly perform, or publicly digitally perform the Work only under the terms of this Licence, and You must include a copy of, or the Uniform Resource Identifier for, this Licence with every copy or phonorecord of the Work You distribute, publicly display, publicly perform, or publicly digitally perform. You may not offer or impose any terms on the Work that alter or restrict the terms of this Licence or the recipients' exercise of the rights granted hereunder. You may not sublicence the Work. You must keep intact all notices that refer to this Licence and to the disclaimer of warranties. You may not distribute, publicly display, publicly perform, or publicly digitally perform the Work with any technological measures that control access or use of the Work in a manner inconsistent with the terms of this Licence Agreement. The above applies to the Work as incorporated in a Collective Work, but this does not require the Collective Work apart from the Work itself to be made subject to the terms of this Licence. If You create a Collective Work, upon notice from any Licencor You must, to the extent practicable, remove from the Collective Work any reference to such Licensor or the Original Author, as requested.
   b   You may not exercise any of the rights granted to You in Section 3 above in any manner that is primarily intended for or directed toward commercial advantage or private monetary

compensation. The exchange of the Work for other copyrighted works by means of digital file-sharing or otherwise shall not be considered to be intended for or directed toward commercial advantage or private monetary compensation, provided there is no payment of any monetary compensation in connection with the exchange of copyrighted works.

c If you distribute, publicly display, publicly perform, or publicly digitally perform the Work or any Collective Works, You must keep intact all copyright notices for the Work and give the Original Author credit reasonable to the medium or means You are utilizing by conveying the name (or pseudonym if applicable) of the Original Author if supplied; the title of the Work if supplied. Such credit may be implemented in any reasonable manner; provided, however, that in the case of a Collective Work, at a minimum such credit will appear where any other comparable authorship credit appears and in a manner at least as prominent as such other comparable authorship credit.

5. Representations, Warranties and Disclaimer

a By offering the Work for public release under this Licence, Licensor represents and warrants that, to the best of Licensor's knowledge after reasonable inquiry:

i Licensor has secured all rights in the Work necessary to grant the licence rights hereunder and to permit the lawful exercise of the rights granted hereunder without You having any obligation to pay any royalties, compulsory licence fees, residuals or any other payments;

ii The Work does not infringe the copyright, trademark, publicity rights, common law rights or any other right of any third party or constitute defamation, invasion of privacy or other tortious injury to any third party.

b EXCEPT AS EXPRESSLY STATED IN THIS LICENCE OR OTHERWISE AGREED IN WRITING OR REQUIRED BY APPLICABLE LAW, THE WORK IS LICENCED ON AN "AS IS" BASIS, WITHOUT WARRANTIES OF ANY KIND, EITHER EXPRESS OR IMPLIED INCLUDING, WITHOUT LIMITATION, ANY WARRANTIES REGARDING THE CONTENTS OR ACCURACY OF THE WORK.

6. Limitation on Liability. EXCEPT TO THE EXTENT REQUIRED BY APPLICABLE LAW, AND EXCEPT FOR DAMAGES ARISING FROM LIABILITY TO A THIRD PARTY RESULTING FROM BREACH OF THE WARRANTIES IN SECTION 5, IN NO EVENT WILL LICENSOR BE LIABLE TO YOU ON ANY LEGAL THEORY FOR ANY SPECIAL, INCIDENTAL, CONSEQUENTIAL, PUNITIVE OR EXEMPLARY DAMAGES ARISING OUT OF THIS LICENCE OR THE USE OF THE WORK, EVEN IF LICENSOR HAS BEEN ADVISED OF THE POSSIBILITY OF SUCH DAMAGES.

7. Termination

a This Licence and the rights granted hereunder will terminate automatically upon any breach by You of the terms of this Licence. Individuals or entities who have received Collective Works from You under this Licence, however, will not have their licences terminated provided such individuals or entities remain in full compliance with those licences. Sections 1, 2, 5, 6, 7, and 8 will survive any termination of this Licence.

b Subject to the above terms and conditions, the licence granted here is perpetual (for the duration of the applicable copyright in the Work). Notwithstanding the above, Licensor reserves the right to release the Work under different licence terms or to stop distributing the Work at any time; provided, however that any such election will not serve to withdraw this Licence (or any other licence that has been, or is required to be, granted under the terms of this Licence), and this Licence will continue in full force and effect unless terminated as stated above.

8. Miscellaneous

a Each time You distribute or publicly digitally perform the Work or a Collective Work, DEMOS offers to the recipient a licence to the Work on the same terms and conditions as the licence granted to You under this Licence.

b If any provision of this Licence is invalid or unenforceable under applicable law, it shall not affect the validity or enforceability of the remainder of the terms of this Licence, and without further action by the parties to this agreement, such provision shall be reformed to the minimum extent necessary to make such provision valid and enforceable.

c No term or provision of this Licence shall be deemed waived and no breach consented to unless such waiver or consent shall be in writing and signed by the party to be charged with such waiver or consent.

d This Licence constitutes the entire agreement between the parties with respect to the Work licensed here. There are no understandings, agreements or representations with respect to the Work not specified here. Licensor shall not be bound by any additional provisions that may appear in any communication from You. This Licence may not be modified without the mutual written agreement of DEMOS and You.